HEALING SPIRITUAL HOMESICKNESS

HEALING SPIRITUAL HOMESICKNESS

a direct path to loving awareness

RADHULE WEININGER, PHD

MANDORLA BOOKS

ISBN: 978-1-950186-62-4

Visit the author's website at www.radhuleweiningerphd.com

Cover design by Benjamin Weininger

MANDORLA BOOKS

PRAISE FOR HEALING SPIRITUAL HOMESICKNESS

To become a profoundly healing and positive presence for others in our world, we must learn how to welcome all of our own painful feelings into a deeply healing environment of warmth and compassion from the ground of our being. Having long trained with leading contemplative teachers of mindfulness, compassion, and wisdom, Radhule Weininger draws her readers into that very process, effectively empowering them to serve on the front lines of care, service and activism.

~John Makransky, developer of
Sustainable Compassion Training,
co-author of *How Compassion Works*

In this book, Radhule Weininger promises wisdom and then skillfully shows how it turns out to be already in us all! I can now see how awareness is not just a form of knowledge but an always accessible holding environment of compassion and loving-kindness. In that "field of care," we come home to a deeper, wider experience of ourselves, of others, and of the world. It takes no special effort; it is available in the "groundless ground" of our very being. I especially liked the "On a Personal Note" sections in each chapter in which Radhule presents us with transparent, close-to-home examples of how we can satisfy our homesickness for the sacred.

~David Richo, PhD, retreat leader, psychotherapist,
and author of numerous books including *By Your Side*

We live in a time of profound longing for a direct way to discover the loving presence that is already here as our true nature. Radhule Weininger, with the rare combination of a scientist's rigor, a psychotherapist's care, a contemplative's depth, and an activist's compassion offers exactly this—a reliable path back to our essential home. Written beautifully and with heart, this book also offers practical ways to directly glimpse the natural compassion and clarity that unites us as a community. Highly recommended!

~Loch Kelly, author of *Shift into Freedom*
and creator of the Mindful Glimpses meditation app

This book is dedicated to my dear friend and mentor, Joanna Macy, whose love and service to the world and all its beings inspired me to do the same

Table of Contents

PART III
LOVE IN ACTION—WHEN HEALING BECOMES SERVICE

FOREWORD

Years ago, I was having a difficult conversation with an old friend. Sitting together in my living room, we were both firmly lodged in our own points of view, and I could feel the tension of our inability to bridge the gap between us. Then, in a moment, my mind did something quite unexpected. Out of the stress of that separation, it suddenly opened to the space that held us both. To my surprise, the energy of that space was a strong and embodied feeling of loving-kindness. This was not something I did, but rather the spontaneous expression of non-separation—a space that is always present, simply waiting to be recognized.

This story came to mind as I was reading Radhule Weininger's remarkable book, *On Spiritual Homesickness*. Through her work as a psychologist and her deep experience in meditation, she has witnessed the suffering that arises from alienation when familiar structures of belonging loosen and from the mistaken perception of a separate self. Although it is easy to see the problem, it is not always clear how to find the way back to a deeper truth: that our true home is not found in external circumstances but in the mindful recognition of the heart's intrinsic clarity and compassion.

In this eminently useful work, Radhule speaks directly to that longing and sense of incompleteness. She offers systematic guidance rooted in ancient Buddhist teachings handed down through centuries of dedicated practitioners. She is a genuine holder of these teachings—deeply practiced and integrated into her life—bringing to this work decades of meditation, clinical insight, and a deeply embodied understanding of the heart's vulnerability and resilience. Through a wealth of personal stories from those she has accompanied over the years, along with profoundly simple exercises and meditation instructions, she shows us the possibility of a lived commitment to compassion, to what she calls "the field of care."

What I appreciate most about this work is its integration of inner realization with compassionate engagement in the world. These are not abstract principles. This book is both a map and an invitation—a way of training the mind and opening the heart so that we can respond to the world without collapsing under its challenges, meeting experience with love and wisdom. I have known Radhule for many years, and her life and her teachings exemplify what is possible for us all.

Joseph Goldstein
Barre, Massachusetts

ACCESS TO AUDIO MEDITATIONS

There are recorded meditations to accompany each of the three parts of the book. You may listen while reading, or allow the practices to stand on their own. Each recording is offered as an invitation to rest in Loving Awareness and deepen your direct experience.

No prior meditation experience is required.

You may access all the mediations at https://www.radhuleweiningerphd.com/spiritual-homesickness-guided-practices

or by using this QR code

INTRODUCTION

Awakening from Spiritual Homesickness

I woke up on a gurney in a narrow hospital corridor. My consciousness hovered in a strange liminal state as I felt a sense of lightness, spaciousness, and silence flowing through me. It was as if a vast, bright field had opened up before me. Everything was calm and still, as if time had paused. My sense of identity and worry had disappeared. For a little while, there was no fear—only a feeling of deep security I had rarely experienced, except perhaps in fleeting moments spent in nature as a young child.

This experience felt both fleeting and endless. I briefly experienced a sense of bliss, clarity, and warmth that I longed for. For a moment, I felt at home. When I opened my eyes and saw several medics standing over me, my normal consciousness returned. As they examined me, I thought, "Oh no, I'm back here again." I had returned to the world I had temporarily left behind.

What I unknowingly discovered in that hospital corridor, and what millions of us desperately need today, is a refuge from what I call "spiritual homesickness"—a deep longing for something more meaningful than what our consumer culture offers, a desire for genuine connection in an increasingly isolated world. While an accident, illness, or loss might open the door for some, others might find a gentler path. Let's find our way home together in a graceful and inspiring manner.

The Epidemic of Our Time

We are facing an unprecedented crisis of meaning. Even though we are more "connected" than any previous generation, millions feel deeply lonely, disconnected from purpose, and homesick for something they can't quite identify. Climate change, political division, violence, and economic instability create a constant sense of anxiety, a lack of basic trust, and a feeling of not belonging in our own lives.

Spiritual homesickness isn't about feeling sad or disappointed with our lives. It's the soul's recognition that we've been separated from our true home—the sacred, or what I call Loving Awareness that shapes our deepest self. Like homesickness for a beloved place, it involves both the pain of separation and the longing for return.

This spiritual displacement appears throughout our modern world.

- **Professionals wonder, "Is this all there is?" despite external success**

  Nathan, CEO of a tech company, feels that his life lacks a spiritual center. He senses a void despite admiration from a wealthy circle of friends and colleagues. Even attending a one-week mindfulness retreat each year does not fill this existential vacuum.

- **Young people searching for meaning in an uncertain world**

  In a meditation group at the local high school, students feel deeply anxious about what the future may bring. There is an uproar in cities at home and abroad over the erosion of the rule of law. Some cannot imagine starting a family. Many seek a deeper sense of security, a home that isn't affected by societal and political changes. They are grieving several of their friends who have taken their own lives.

- **Healthcare workers experiencing moral injury and seeking purpose**

Mora, a nurse at a local clinic, feels heartbroken watching the fate of many of her undocumented patients. Little Anna is alone with a fractured arm, after her mom was taken by ICE. Mora doesn't know how to cope with her sadness.

- **Climate activists facing eco-anxiety and spiritual despair**

  Tina, a young environmental scientist, feels hopeless and overwhelmed, believing that restoring the climate's balance and nature is slipping further away. She feels isolated and disconnected from society.

- **Millions are feeling "connection without connection" through technology**

  Mark and Lucia, two young computer programmers, feel completely cut off. All their connections are online, and both of them sense that something is seriously wrong.

- **Parents of young children who balance kids, marriage, and work life**

  Ram and Sally, parents of two boys, are desperately trying to keep their lives afloat financially, tending to their kids' needs while trying to maintain their own relationship.

- **The ongoing feeling that "there must be more to life than this"**

  Sarah, a 79-year-old retired schoolteacher, feels that her life is lacking meaning and friends. For months, she has been having trouble sleeping at night.

The Triple Disconnection

Through decades of practice, study, and working with thousands of people as a psychologist and teacher, I've found that spiritual homesickness comes from a threefold separation:

Disconnection from our true nature (the ground of being) causes us to lose contact with the endless source of love and awareness that is our deepest identity, leaving us spiritually drained.

Disconnection from our fundamental interconnectedness and kinship with others causes us to lose sight of our essential unity with all life and the ground of being. This disconnection has led to the isolation and loneliness that define our digitally hyperconnected yet spiritually empty age.

Disconnection from our authentic purpose—our true service—has led us to become distant from work and relationships that naturally grow from love. This leaves us exhausted from constant effort, driven solely by willpower. Connecting to the ground and the field of Loving Awareness gives us deep resilience, which sustains meaningful engagement.

The Three-Part Medicine

What kick-started my journey down that hospital corridor—and what this book reveals—is that these three disconnections can all be healed at once through what I call the "triple medicine":

Non-dual awareness and sustainable compassion practices help us recognize the deep loving ground of being, which provides endless energy and nourishment for living well.

Resting in the ground of being gives us deep resilience. This allows us to realize our fundamental interconnectedness. We can now access the warmth and wisdom that heals the loneliness at the core of spiritual homesickness.

Sustainable engaged service, as a genuine expression of love and interconnectedness, offers real meaning and purpose. Our engagement is now energized by the foundation of being, protecting us from overwhelm and burnout.

When these three come together, spiritual homesickness isn't just healed—it's transformed into the very solution our world needs: people who serve selflessly from an endless source, connected in love, and filled with true purpose.

- Five times per week, from 7:30-8:00 a.m., our non-profit Mindfulheartprograms.org offers an online meditation for free. Sarah started meditating and joined our group. As this event is ongoing, she got acquainted with the other 10-12 visitors to this group. She also began teaching English to 8- to 10-year-olds twice a week at the local library. When I see her, she tells me that she is happy. She feels connected with life again and spiritually at peace.

"There is a crack in everything; that's how the light gets in" (Leonard Cohen)

A severe existential crisis led to the accident that woke me up in the hospital corridor. I had crashed into a streetlight. Life in post-war Germany felt empty, dominated by consumerism and the lingering shadows of war. The fateful accident tore a hole in the barrier separating different levels of reality. This crack allowed light to enter, initially as a trickle, then as a flood of brightness and warmth.

I was 23 years old when my childhood trauma and existential wounds compelled me to seek psychological and spiritual healing. I started meditating in Sri Lanka, including spending several months in a forest monastery. What began as personal desperation became a lifelong dedication to making the healing I found accessible to others experiencing similar spiritual confusion. The current moment we are living through, with its existential uncertainties, reminds me of the confusion and pain all those years ago.

However, now, four and a half decades after this pivotal accident, I am now in my 68th year and coming to the later years of my professional and personal life. I realize how freeing it was to be pushed to explore the depths of the abyss and find the light within. *(On a*

Personal Note: see below)[1] What I learned, and what many of us desperately need today, is a refuge—a home that doesn't depend on external circumstances or years of tedious practice.

Who Are You? How Are You Suffering?

You picked up this book because something inside you senses a spiritual homesickness. Maybe you've experienced moments of expanded awareness that opened you up—peak experiences in nature, flow states, unexpected insights during meditation—but like most of us, you've struggled to sustain these moments. They come as gifts and then fade, leaving you wondering how to find your way back home.

Maybe you're one of many who feel overwhelmed by today's complex crises: political division, economic instability, violence, the possible rise of fascism, often mixed with personal pain. The post-pandemic world has left millions wrestling with a vague death anxiety and deep questions they've been avoiding through busyness and distraction.

Even when everything around you feels sufficient, you might still experience a sense of inner homelessness—a lack of purpose that manifests as fatigue, aimlessness, or a constant feeling that you're just going through the motions of a life that doesn't truly nourish your soul. You might feel an inner void and struggle to connect with something essential and meaningful.

This isn't a personal failure. This deep longing for something we can't quite define, along with a subtle feeling of dissatisfaction, is a natural response to living in a world that has lost touch with its

---

[1] ***On a Personal Note:*** *It took me much emotional and spiritual work to free myself from the cocoon of a disapproving and narrow-minded family back in Germany. Gradually, I found a place where I could discover who I was and follow my calling towards an unfolding path as a passionate mother and wife, a psychotherapist, author, meditation teacher, and workshop leader. It was hard and rewarding to free myself from these emotional, relational bondages, so I could become a spiritually clear, socially engaged and, most of all, open-hearted person.*

spiritual core. Our disconnection from meaning, others, and the natural world has left millions of us feeling like exiles in our own lives.

Be a Spiritual Rebel

Here's what I've learned as someone who started with deep alienation and spiritual hunger: After years of seeking, learning from remarkable teachers, and working as a psychologist, activist, and mystic, I realized that many people practice secular mindfulness but have lost the sacred. It's become dry and only practical. Or, to experience the sacred, others feel they have to join religious institutions that don't align with their authentic selves.

Be a spiritual rebel. You don't need to join anything or adopt beliefs that don't fit your life. You don't have to spend years in monasteries or decades on meditation cushions waiting for the sacred to reveal itself.

What you need are the most effective non-dual awareness practices that are accessible and relevant—practices that directly point to the awakened state, fostering immediate recognition and helping you sustain it. These pointing-out practices are reliable methods for healing spiritual homesickness and rediscovering the sacred in everyday life.

Think of this as a GPS guiding you home to the field of love and awareness that has always been your true nature.

The Medicine Our World Needs

This isn't just about personal healing. As social and environmental activist and Buddhist scholar Joanna Macy taught me: "Only as we feel our pain for this world can we feel our love for it fully." When we recognize and heal our own spiritual homesickness, we naturally become medicine for our collectively spiritually displaced world.

The exercises in this book establish a structured approach for this transformation.

- **Part I** explores spiritual homesickness by reconnecting us with the essence of being itself, demonstrating that awareness's natural qualities include care, warmth, and love alongside its inherent wisdom. These are not merely comforting techniques we add to awareness meditation, but a recognition of the loving nature that awareness already holds.

- **Part II** deepens and stabilizes our understanding of true nature while clearly pointing out our essential interconnectedness.

- **Part III** illustrates how awakening naturally evolves into sustainable service—love and compassion transform into active engagement without burnout, offering the meaning and purpose that ultimately resolves spiritual homesickness.

What You're Really Seeking

What I discovered in that hospital corridor, and what you're truly searching for, isn't another spiritual technique or philosophy. It's the understanding that you already are what you've been seeking. This journey isn't about adding something new; it's about recognizing what has always been here, possibly overlooked during our hectic search for something significant outside ourselves.

When we shift from a limited, separate sense of self to recognizing our true nature as boundless Loving Awareness, we heal the spiritual homesickness that causes much modern suffering. We realize that we are not isolated individuals trying to find meaning in an indifferent universe; we are expressions of love and awareness itself, inherently connected to all life and called to serve from this awareness.

Our Collective Assignment

My dear friend Joanna Macy, who died peacefully in 2025 at age 96, captured why this path matters now in our spiritually homesick world when she and Betsy Omdahl wrote:

Sky may fall and the mountains too,
Seas may rise, and the wind blows through,
I got a job to do.

Gotta keep loving in a world of pain,
We got a job to do.

In times of great existential anxiety and confusion around values as well as widespread spiritual displacement, we need dependable access to something deeper than our reactive patterns or fleeting comforts. This path isn't about escaping our spiritually homesick world; it's about engaging with it through expansive, openhearted awareness that transforms everything it touches.

The practices in this book will teach you how to access this realm of love and wisdom consistently and reliably in your daily life. You'll find the refuge that has always been here, waiting for you to return to your spiritual home—and in finding your way back, you'll become a guide for others on the same journey.

Welcome to a journey that heals spiritual homesickness by showing it was never an illness but a call to remember who you really are.

PART I

HEALING THE ROOTS OF SPIRITUAL HOMESICKNESS

QR Code for the Audio for Practices in Part I

or visit https://www.radhuleweiningerphd.com/spiritual-homesick-ness-part-one

CHAPTER 1

Living in a Spiritually Homesick World

We are facing an epidemic of spiritual homesickness. Many, like Aaron, a family lawyer and father of two, wake up at 3 or 4 a.m., their nervous systems stirred by a vague yet persistent sense that something is deeply wrong—not just on an individual level, but collectively. This isn't a personal failure; it is the natural result of living disconnected from the Field of Love in a world that has forgotten its own spiritual nature.

Digital Displacement and the Achievement Paradox

In our hyperconnected yet lonely world, spiritual homesickness manifests as the strange feeling of being more isolated despite constant digital connection and feeling empty inside, even with external success. This is what I call the "achievement paradox"—the more we meet society's standards, the more spiritually disconnected we often feel.

The post-pandemic world has deepened this collective spiritual reflection. Millions who once found purpose in busy routines, career growth, and social activities have realized that when these external structures disappeared, they faced a significant spiritual emptiness. The "quiet quitting" phenomenon shows not only dissatisfaction at work but also a deeper spiritual craving—a recognition that traditional success measures don't fulfill the soul.

Modern symptoms of spiritual homesickness include:

- Constantly staying busy to fill an inner void
- Addiction to Devices and Distractions

- Political anger which, though understandable, hides a deeper longing for care and connection
- Climate anxiety, lacking spiritual grounding
- A success that feels empty despite external achievements
- Superficial relationships despite "connections" on social media
- The ongoing sense that "there must be more to life than this"

Officer Maria Rodriguez had been patrolling the downtown beat for eight years, her badge a shield against the chaos of human suffering she faced every day. She had learned to compartmentalize, keeping her compassion locked away during shift hours, allowing it to surface only in the privacy of her apartment. There, she would weep for the homeless woman who had died alone or the teenager caught stealing formula for his baby sister.

Like many people in our spiritually homesick world, Maria had learned to separate her professional self from her caring heart, not realizing that this very separation was part of what left her feeling empty despite her dedication to service.

The call came in at 11:47 p.m.: a domestic disturbance on Maple Street. Maria's partner, Jake, was already reaching for his radio, calling for backup. "Third time this month," he muttered. "Danny's drinking again."

Maria knew the address well. Danny Mitchell, who had recently been laid off from the factory, had three kids under ten, and his wife was working double shifts to make ends meet. The pattern was predictable: alcohol, argument, neighbors calling out of fear, arrest, temporary restraining order, and then the cycle started all over again.

As they pulled up, Maria saw the familiar scene through the window—Danny towering over his wife, Catherine, fists clenched, and the children huddled on the couch. Her training kicked in: assess the threat, establish control, remove the aggressor, and protect the victims. Precise, efficient, and by the book.

But something held her back at the doorway. Maybe it was the way Danny's shoulders were trembling, or how Catherine's eyes showed not just fear but deep exhaustion—the kind that comes from loving someone who's drowning and not knowing how to save them.

Maria had been practicing something her meditation teacher called "resting in the field of Loving Awareness"—a way of accessing a deeper consciousness that seemed to intuitively understand what was needed at each moment. It had started as a survival technique during her most difficult cases, but it had become something much more powerful. Instead of her usual adrenaline-fueled approach, she found herself dropping into that vast, still space she had been learning to trust.

Taking a slow breath, she felt her feet on the ground, her heart pounding in her chest, and then—that familiar expansion, like stepping into a cathedral of awareness. From this place, she could see Danny not just as a threat to be neutralized, but as a man whose world had fallen apart, whose sense of purpose had been stripped away along with his paycheck. This understanding wasn't analytical; it arose spontaneously from the field of love itself.

"Danny," she said softly, entering the room with her hands visible and empty. "I know you're hurting."

The words surprised even her. Jake shot her a look, but she kept going, her voice both firm and gentle. "I can see you love your family. That's why this is tearing you apart."

Danny's fists loosened just a bit. His bloodshot, wild eyes finally locked on hers. "You don't understand," he whispered. "I can't even feed them."

I understand," Maria said sincerely. "But scaring them won't feed them either. And they need their dad—the real you, not this version that the pain has created."

What happened next defied her training manual. Danny's knees buckled, and he sank into a chair, his head in his hands. Catherine moved toward him—not away—and gently placed a hand on his shoulder. The children left the couch and quietly crept closer.

Maria realized she was witnessing something her years of enforcement had rarely seen: a moment when wisdom and compassion create space for healing instead of just managing damage. She was still a police officer, still responsible for safety, but now she was acting as a bridge between punishment and possibility.

"Let's figure out how to help," she said, pulling out her phone to call not just the crisis counselor, but the job placement service, the food bank, and the AA meeting schedule. "All of us, together."

For the first time in years, Maria felt the full power of her greatest asset—not her training or her weapon, but her ability to rest in that field of love. This wasn't just about maintaining peace; it was about tapping into what felt like a superpower—the ability to create space where transformation could happen naturally. Her meditation practice had shown her that conscious love in action was the most fundamental creative force available to her, and tonight she trusted it completely.

She wasn't just helping to create the conditions where peace could flourish—she was drawing from the very source of peace itself, allowing it to flow through her into a situation that desperately needed healing, delivering the medicine this family, along with our spiritually homesick world, desperately needs.

From Personal Healing to Collective Medicine

As we heal our own spiritual homesickness through these practices, we naturally become sources of healing for others facing similar disconnection. Maria's transformation enabled her to serve others experiencing comparable spiritual displacement—offering a healing presence to those who, like Danny, had lost their sense of purpose and belonging. Her story exemplifies the core promise of this book: when we access Loving Awareness, all three aspects of spiritual homesickness are healed at once—we connect with the boundless source, recognize our unity with all life, and serve from love effortlessly without burning out.

When Wisdom and Compassion Come Together

When wisdom and compassion unify in awareness, they generate what could be called a "sacred resonance," a vibration that surpasses the sum of its parts. This isn't just simple addition; it's a step into a new realm of being and acting that fundamentally transforms how we connect with existence, bringing healing to our spiritually homesick world.

The hand of wisdom provides clarity, discernment, and the ability to see through illusions with precision. It offers the sharp light of understanding that cuts through confusion, revealing what is truly essential at any moment. However, wisdom alone can feel cold, detached, even clinical—a brilliant light without warmth.

The hand of compassion offers warmth, connection, and the magnetic pull of love that draws us to ease suffering wherever it exists. It provides an embracing quality that includes all beings within its care, holding them with boundless tenderness. However, compassion alone can become overwhelming, unfocused, or even enabling—a warm embrace without clear direction.

When these two hands come together in Namaste, something remarkable happens: wisdom is illuminated by love, and compassion is guided by clarity. The result is what you might call "skillful love" or "loving wisdom," a force that is gentle and precise, embracing and discerning, fierce and tender all at once.

This alchemical fusion creates what spiritual traditions refer to as "awakened heart"—the heart that naturally cares for the well-being of all beings. It is not an emotional state that shifts like the weather, but a steady awareness of our fundamental interconnectedness, fueled by the limitless power of awareness itself.

When this unified intention encounters another person, it creates a space of mutual recognition—suddenly, both beings are immersed in the vast realm of knowing love. When it interacts with a group, it can spark collective awakening, sending ripples outward in waves of transformation. When it engages with our spiritually homesick world, it becomes a healing force that works not through force or manipulation but through the compelling power of truth and love united in service.

This is truly a superpower—not in terms of supernatural abilities, but in recognizing that we have access to the most fundamental creative force in the universe: conscious love in action. From this place, our mission isn't something we struggle to accomplish against resistance, but something that naturally flows from our deepest nature, carried by the current of life itself toward its highest expression. *(On a Personal Note: see below)*[2]

Beyond Ordinary Mindfulness: The Direct Path

You might know about mindfulness, but there's a big difference between traditional mindfulness and the non-dual practices we'll discuss in this book.

Traditional mindfulness helps calm our minds and open our hearts. By paying attention to bodily sensations, thoughts, and feelings, we can achieve a calm and peaceful state. Attending extended silent retreats helps us better understand how our minds work.

While mindfulness retreats promote insight through careful observation, understanding impermanence, and detachment, non-dual practices introduce something entirely new. They directly point to the awakened state, encouraging immediate recognition and letting us rest in it. These practices provide a direct path home from spiritual homesickness.

Non-dual practices come from contemplative traditions around the world. They teach us to recognize and stay in the space of awareness itself by learning to remain in what's called the "natural state of mind" or "Loving Awareness."

Think of it this way: traditional mindfulness is like hiking a mountain trail step by step for a long time, while non-dual practices are similar to gently floating in a balloon that brings you closer to

---

[2] ***On a Personal Note:*** *It was a monumental discovery that wisdom and compassion could be equal parts of my practice, which complemented each other. When I lived in the Sri Lankan Black Rock Monastery in 1981 for some months, compassion was not an important part of how we practiced. Compassion was mentioned, but wisdom and understanding of how things really are were at the core. Even though I was enthusiastic to learn, something felt a bit cold, rigid, very strict, and somehow disembodied.*

When I discovered years later kindness and compassion through Sharon Salzberg's beautiful practices, I was able to go much deeper into the meditation experience. There was now, besides wisdom, a warmth for myself and the world.

the summit. Both methods ultimately reach the goal, but the "direct path" might be easier and more relevant for many of us living busy, complicated modern lives in a spiritually homesick world. *(On a Personal Note: see below)*[3]

The Teachers Who Shaped This Path

This book draws wisdom from several extraordinary teachers who have shaped my understanding, along with my own voice as a psychologist, activist, and mystic. I am someone who longs to access the deepest core and bring it forth so it can shine through our engagement with a wounded, spiritually longing world.

I offer a feminine perspective grounded in gentleness and love for our world, including its children, animals, and especially nature. Over my 25 years as an author and teacher, I have felt a deep desire to connect the wisdom of mostly male non-dual teachers with everyday life as a friend, mother, caregiver, and wife. More than 30 years of listening to my clients as a psychotherapist have provided me with a deep understanding of the human mind, strong empathy for human suffering, and insight into how psychological and spiritual healing work together. I have found a language that is not

---

[3] ***On a Personal Note:*** *For me, learning about non-dual awareness and instructions that would point me to a direct and authentic experience of the deep ground of being was monumental. With these practices, I did not have to wait for the long retreat six months away to have a strong spiritual feeling. Instead, I was now able to not only be immersed in the sacred, but also become an aspect of Loving Awareness. It was as if I were having a different operating system, as if I were living from a different perspective.*

When seeing my clients, I then felt that I didn't need to the therapist "fixing them," but that I could provide an open and loving environment in which healing could just happen. When teaching meditation, I did not have to pump myself up as a meditation teacher, but the teaching and guiding would just come through me. When reading the news, danger, violence, and fear were no longer the "bottom line." They were now passing phenomena held in the vast experience of life. The sadness about cruelty and suffering remains, but the pain is held in Loving Awareness.

abstract but speaks directly to our hearts—a way of teaching that is accessible and meaningful.

Buddhist scholar and teacher John Makransky showed how to see the field of awareness as a "Field of Care," emphasizing the love quality naturally present in non-dual awareness. His approach, called "sustainable compassion," serves as both protection and nourishment, helping us hold vulnerable feelings with gentle presence. When our emotions are received, included, and protected, we learn to trust and can become a "Field of Care" for others in our spiritually homesick world.

Daniel P. Brown, a meditation teacher and therapist, demonstrated how to intentionally and reliably access the field of awareness. Dan's "Pointing Out Instructions" serve as a GPS to Loving Awareness, providing a consistent method to reach and ultimately stabilize this expansive perspective, which I rarely experienced before. The field of Loving Awareness can gradually develop into a new way of seeing—a new operating system that infuses and guides our lives.

Loch Kelly, a meditation teacher and psychotherapist, turned these practices into short "glimpses" that smoothly fit into daily routines, which you can experience at his Mindful Glimpses app. These quick exercises, sometimes only seconds long, make this approach accessible to everyone, no matter how busy they are. These glimpses supplement Daniel Brown's longer, more detailed practices. They help us stay mindful throughout the day.

The psychologist and insight meditation teacher Jack Kornfield has been teaching me for three decades that meditation, psychology, and social engagement are all parts of the same spiritual practice. Through his gentle mentoring, he has shown me how to serve others and our world.

Joanna Macy, who loved this world and its creatures, inspired the heart of this book. Her teaching that only our ability to feel with the pain of the world can fully open our hearts, is burnt into my soul. The understanding that our compassion for the deep suffering of our world allows us to love it, has shown itself to be absolutely true to me. When we grasp the interconnectedness of all life, everything becomes worthy of our care—and we become healers for our spiritually homesick world. *(On a Personal Note: see below)*[4]

Your Journey Begins Here

Many of us have experienced flow states—subtle forms of alert awareness—during childhood or later in life. These moments might happen in nature, where time suddenly feels unimportant, or during activities like sports, playing music, creating art, surfing, or other peak experiences. They offer glimpses of what we will explore in more detail—brief returns home from spiritual homesickness.

Take a moment to reflect: How did you get here today? What questions are on your mind? What is the true essence of your longing? If you'd like, spend some time journaling.

Many of us ponder big questions about life. Why am I here? What truly matters? What values give my life meaning? Is it only safety,

---

[4] ***On a Personal Note:*** *There are mentors who diligently taught me practices, methods, and Buddhist philosophy, and there are teachers who followed me with their gentle companionship, guidance, and maybe transmission of a way of being. The first of such heart mentors was Bante Dhamaloka, the head of a Buddhist sect, whom I met completely unexpectedly when I stumbled into his monastery during a monsoon storm. Sitting in front of him, I felt, to my surprise, a completely different reality in utter stillness, lucidity, and bliss. I experienced profound awe and knew that this would be my path for life.*

Jack Kornfield has lovingly mentored me by now for 25 years. He has guided me through the storms of divorce, professional challenges, and philosophical doubts on this curvy path to freedom.

Joanna Macy was my close friend for 15 years; her love has carried me forward. She helped me to bring Theravada and Mahayana, social activism and the contemplative path together, by just spending lots of time in her kitchen, sitting room and in the forest together. She taught me that nothing matters without loving the world.

Joseph Goldstein has been a friend for only a few years. Jimmie, a homeless monk with an addiction problem, became our bridge. Taking care of Jimmie together made it clear that this path is about suffering and the freedom from suffering, with hands-on care and gentleness.

comfort, and personal growth that count, or do I also seek a sense of purpose that cares for others? How many people do I choose to care for: my family, community, country, those far away, animals, or the earth?

Take a moment to reflect: How have you shaped your current values? What questions do you carry with you? What is at the heart of your longing for home?

Simple Practice: Feeling Your Longing

Time needed: 5 minutes

Purpose: Clarify the deeper longing that brought you to this path—this practice offers healing from spiritual homesickness by helping you recognize the soul's call to return home.

Instructions:

1. Pick a quiet and comfortable place to sit.
2. Feel your body touch the chair and the ground.
3. Notice your mood: Are you feeling comfortable, uncomfortable, or neutral?
4. Listen inwardly to recognize a longing, which might be for peace of mind, peace of heart, an experience of the boundless sacred, connection to others, a sense of belonging to an interconnected web of life, or a desire for meaning and purpose.
5. Simply describe this yearning inside you—notice if it feels like homesickness for something you can't quite name.

Maybe this exercise helps you realize that you're not the only one searching for home; perhaps home, the groundless ground, the great mystery, is also longing for you.

Integration:

Remember, this journey isn't about introducing something new; it's about noticing what has always been there, perhaps overlooked. It's something we carry inside us that we can shine into our spiritually homesick world.

As the contemplative woman teacher Naguma said a thousand years ago:

- This close, you can't see it.
- This deep, you can't fathom it.
- This simple, you can't believe it.
- This good, you can't accept it.
- Yet, it is only a moment of remembering away.

What Lies Ahead

It might be a relatively new idea to view non-dual awareness practices as a way to support a fulfilling life and heal our collective spiritual homesickness. Today, mindfulness has shifted from being a spiritual practice to a practical tool for stress relief, mental health, and other purposes. Non-dual awareness practices, which were once mainly for monks seeking enlightenment, are now accessible to help us manage the many tasks needed to keep our spiritually homesick world on a healthy, balanced path.

We are lucky to be alive during this important time when practices once hidden are now available to help us navigate the tough journey ahead in healing our personal and collective spiritual homesickness.

In the upcoming chapters, we will embark on this entire journey, from opening the heart through the Field of Care to developing the focus that helps us recognize Loving Awareness, and then integrating this awareness into a life of active compassion. Each chapter builds on the previous one, creating a steady path back to your true nature—a journey home from spiritual homesickness.

This journey begins with one step: being open to the idea that what you've been searching for has been here all along.

CHAPTER 2

The Field of Care—Opening the Heart and Touching the Ground of Being

These teachers and practices are essential now because, as Aaron, the lawyer and father of two, discovered at 4:15 a.m., we all face moments when our usual coping strategies break down. During personal crises or global uncertainties, we need more than just positive thoughts or distractions; we need a foundation rooted in being itself. This is when the Field of Care becomes not just helpful but crucial—especially in a world where we feel spiritually homesick.

This practice offers healing for spiritual homesickness by reconnecting us with the first aspect of the triple medicine: touching the ground of being itself. What we find is revolutionary—awareness isn't cold or neutral but inherently warm, caring, and loving. This isn't about adding heartwarming practices to awareness; it's about recognizing that the field of awareness already has qualities of care, warmth, and love alongside its natural wisdom.

When Aaron woke up at 4:15 a.m., his heart was pounding against his ribs—fast, irregular, and relentless—another sleepless night in what seemed like an endless string of them. He wasn't alone. In our spiritually lost world, millions of people wake up at this hour, their nervous systems stirred by a vague yet persistent sense that something is terribly wrong—not just personally, but collectively and spiritually.

Taking a deep breath was tough for Aaron. During those moments, holding onto something steady brought temporary comfort. His partner stirred, softly placed her hand on his, and whispered, "Awake again? We have work tomorrow, and the kids will be up at 7 a.m." For weeks, Aaron, like many of us, had been waking before dawn, anxious about what the coming weeks and months might bring. "Try to sleep," she murmured.

In the darkness, old ghosts moved along their silent, relentless paths. Images from his family history surfaced: his grandfather facing violence for speaking the truth in an authoritarian country, and friends working in conflict zones with worried eyes. In his mind's eye, he saw them witnessing suffering, their bodies physically showing the stress. His mind conjured images of limited healthcare access, unfair judicial systems, and families living in fear. A question haunted him: Is this truly 2026? Nearly a century had passed since a major crisis engulfed Europe and the world, yet the echoes felt disturbingly familiar. He thought of his own little sons—what lives will they have, will they have to fight in wars, will there be a healthy planet when they grow up?

Aaron's anxiety wasn't just personal stress; it was spiritual homesickness—a deep feeling that something essential was missing from his life and our collective world. This restless search for meaning and the sense of disconnection, despite being more "connected" than any previous generation, highlights the epidemic of spiritual homesickness spreading through our modern world.

In these moments, we seek refuge from relentless thoughts and feelings. The "Field of Care" practice, created by teacher John Makransky, offers deep relief. This practice encourages us to recall instances of true care—perhaps sitting with friends in a sacred space, bathed in honey-colored light, and feeling fully loved and safe. By remembering the sensation of such moments, loving qualities emerge from our core awareness—not as something we produce, but as something we recognize. Care, warmth, acceptance, and being deeply seen come naturally. A sense of inner peace, safety, well-being, tenderness, and openness becomes accessible.

We can embrace these qualities and align ourselves with them. Practicing this meditation during moments of distress, along with our daily routine, provides reliable relief. More importantly, consistently practicing the Field of Care helps us experience Loving Awareness as a natural and essential part of being human. This refuge in the Field of Care becomes critical if we want to continue caring for others during difficult times—and if we want to bring healing to our wounded world.

The Heart as Gateway to Awakening

The heart represents both the start and end of our spiritual journey. That's why it's crucial to connect with our hearts before beginning a journey to discover Loving Awareness—especially when we're working to heal spiritual homesickness.

Many Eastern traditions speak of the Heart-Mind. I see this as an energetic rather than a physical space where our personal awareness connects with the universal field, awakening the heart. Most of us face complex challenges in our daily lives. Wisdom and compassion—qualities of an awakened heart—give us the strength to find creative, intelligent, and loving ways forward. An awakened heart creates the foundation for our awareness practices and guides us in finding our way home while serving life.

Beginning our practice by recognizing the inherent care within awareness calms the wandering or restless mind. Just as a frightened child relaxes when held by a caring parent, our restless thoughts and emotions settle when embraced by the "Field of Care." This practice helps our nervous systems feel balanced and secure by reconnecting us with the loving nature of awareness itself.

Christian mystic Cynthia Bourgeau reminds us that our Heart-Mind is the point where our personal awareness connects with the universal field of awareness. By learning to recognize and accept the love that is already present within awareness, we activate a healing power that has always been available to us. The simple act of allowing ourselves to be embraced by this Field of Care can change how we see the world, opening us to an inner wisdom that appreciates the fundamental goodness of being.

The Mother-Child Connection in Spiritual Practice

From a non-dual perspective, our Heart-Mind serves as the connection between our personal "child-consciousness" and the universal "mother-consciousness" of Loving Awareness. Interestingly, modern Western psychology also employs the "mother-child" metaphor.

Whether we explore self-psychology, attachment theory, or internal family systems, a child's relationship with their mother (or primary caregiver) is crucial for developing secure bonds, trusting themselves and others, and building emotional resilience during tough times.

Many factors influence a person's development, and there are various ways to heal old wounds. I faced a difficult early childhood and needed creative methods to heal and grow. *(On a Personal Note: see below)*[5] When I first trained as a psychologist, long-term therapy was the only treatment considered valid. However, I realized that spiritual and psychological healing methods complement each other. Such healing can lead to what is called "earned secure attachment"—we can "earn" healing through our connection to a loving person and to loving, awake, compassionate awareness itself. Eventually, we realize that we ourselves are a spark of Loving Awareness. After my car accident, I found that, besides psychotherapy, connecting spiritually to the ground of being was essential for healing my wounds.

---

[5] ***On a Personal Note:*** *Growing up in post-war Germany with a single mother, and a Catholic, judgmental family observing me with critical eyes, I had a lot of psychological work to do to handle deep feelings of shame and inferiority. This deep psychological work became vastly enhanced when I began to feel held in an atmosphere of goodness—I felt that Loving Awareness as a direct and true experience was "having my back."*

Field of Care Practice

(adapted from John Makransky)

Core Concept

The Field of Care Practice serves as the foundation for John's Sustainable Compassion practices. It helps us experience awareness as a "Field of Care" that already embodies warmth and compassion, as well as its timeless, formless, indestructible, and luminous nature. By recalling supportive figures who showed us genuine care, we can evoke and access these compassionate qualities that have always existed within the very nature of awareness—offering the first medicine for spiritual homesickness.

Practice 1: Touching the Field of Care

Time needed: 1-2 minutes

Purpose: Experience a brief glimpse of the Field of Care—this practice answers to our spiritual longing by connecting us with the inherent loving nature of awareness

1. Ground yourself: Feel your body sitting or lying down
2. Connect with a memory: Recall a person who made you feel safe, acknowledged, or loved
3. Embody the feeling: Feel that sense of care in your body right now
4. Release the memory and remain immersed in the felt sense of the experience
5. Breathe with it: Hold this sensation for 3 to 4 breaths
6. Notice the shift: See how this subtly alters your state

Integration: This simple practice can be used anytime you want to reconnect with a sense of safety and care—especially when spiritual homesickness feels overwhelming.

Practice 2: Field of Care Foundation

Time needed: 10-15 min

Purpose: Build a stable connection to Loving Awareness as a foundation for all other practices—establishing a sense of belonging and spiritual home by recognizing awareness as inherently caring

Preparation:

- Relax into your body, staying both upright and at ease
- Shift your awareness from your thinking mind to your whole-body sensations
- Allow your body to rest as awareness, and let awareness rest as the body

Core Practice: Connect with Breath

- Feel the breath naturally arise and dissolve back into the body
- Let yourself be drawn into the gap between in-breath and out-breath
- Allow this to open into the field-quality of awareness

Invoke Care

- From these depths, let an image of a caring figure emerge
- This could be a loved one, a friend, a stranger, an animal, a place in nature, a mentor, or a spiritual figure
- Feel the sensation of this moment of care as it happens right now

Receive Care

- Be open to loving energy filling your body and mind
- Let it satiate every part of you, down to each cell, layer of feeling, and emotion

- Feel each part of your being deeply cherished in its true essence.
- Let the memory fade and fully experience the essence of that moment
- Rest in the felt sense of your memory

Hold All Experience

- Allow thoughts or feelings to remain in this loving space if they arise
- Every part of you, including any sense of spiritual longing, is loved in its essence
- Return to the feeling of that moment of care and fully relax into it

Expand into Spaciousness

- Allow yourself to fully immerse in this loving energy.
- Let your awareness fully and freely flow into the vast, boundless space
- Rest in awareness, as awareness

Reflection: Feel this practice in your body, heart, and mind

Key Insight

The many moments of love and care around us each day often go unnoticed. As we learn to pay closer attention to these acts of kindness, we begin to see our deep connection to a web of benevolence that has always been there. With consistent practice, this can grow from a personal, intentional act into one that you "live without doing." At that point, you become the Field of Care, and the Field of Care becomes you—offering healing presence to our spiritually homesick world. *(On a Personal Note: see below)*[6]

---

[6] ***On a Personal Note:*** *In my own experience, when I began to truly internalize the feeling that a Field of Care is always present, my*

The Source of Sustainable Compassion

Something remarkable happens when our compassion flows from an awake heart rather than from a sense of obligation or effortful striving: we don't experience exhaustion. There's no "compassion fatigue," "empathic distress," or burnout. Our love and care well up naturally, like clear water from an underground spring that never runs dry.

I've realized that the source of our love, compassion, generosity, and forgiveness isn't something we need to create. It comes from what I sometimes call the "groundless ground" that exists within and beyond everything we can imagine. This source of life is vast, limitless, and deeply nurturing—the very antidote to spiritual homesickness.

Field of Care as a Receptacle for All Our Experiences

Realizing that the Field of Care is an experience we can access—a space that embraces our feelings, thoughts, and even uncomfortable emotions within a broad, caring, and nurturing environment—is truly inspiring.

After we start by recalling and embodying a loving, supportive moment from our lives, our capacity for unconditional love deepens. Our ability to accept and embrace our own feelings of discomfort or doubt, as well as the suffering of others, becomes easier. As we experience the profound security and healing power of this renewed sense of care and acceptance, we no longer need to avoid or reject what feels uncomfortable. Instead, our minds become willing to release what is painful into openness and warmth. What has been tangled up can now begin to untangle itself.

This is especially important for those experiencing themselves as spiritually lost—instead of rejecting or trying to fix these feelings of disconnection and longing, we can hold them with the same loving care we would offer a hurt child.

---

relationship to my environment and other people began to change significantly. I was able to be more generous and tolerant towards others, to forgive more easily, and to feel gratitude.

Practice: Compassionate Presence to Feelings

(adapted from John Makransky)

Time needed: 10-15 min

Purpose of practice: Embrace your feelings compassionately so they can relax and dissolve naturally—healing spiritual homesickness by creating a loving space for all experiences

Preparation:

- Let yourself settle into your body as a whole
- Feel your whole-body sense of feeling
- Feel your breath rise and dissolve naturally, all on its own

Establish Field of Care

- Remember your Field of Care, whether it is a person, a pet, nature, or a spiritual figure you felt loved by
- Stay with the felt sense of that experience for a moment before letting go of the specific memory
- Stay with that feeling in your body

Working With Physical Discomfort

- After a while, pay attention to any physical discomfort in your body
- Become aware of it in an open and accepting way
- And let it find its own way of settling in
- In time, it will change and dissolve

Working with Emotions

- Now, sense what emotional feeling is in your body
- Feel what you feel from the inside out

- There might be some anxiety, doubt in the practice, numbness, or something very subtle
- Or you might experience a stronger emotion like fear, frustration, fear of missing out, or shame
- Notice if there's a spiritual ache—that deep longing for something more meaningful
- As you become aware of those feelings with a deep sense of permission, fully allow them to be there, without judging or rejecting them
- Rest with that feeling in openness, and allow it to settle into its own place, until it dissolves or changes all by itself

Integration

- Let your awareness fully open to infinite, boundless space
- Let yourself fully relax into this loving energy
- Rest in awareness, as awareness

Reflection: Feel this practice in your body, heart, and mind

Key Insight

Instead of isolating ourselves from difficult feelings, we learn to allow them to serve as a way to connect when held within the Field of Care.

Often, we don't know how to handle the discomfort inside ourselves or others. We usually learn to avoid, suppress, distract, detach, or deny it. But doing so keeps us stuck in suffering and stops us from being free. With a strong foundation in caring, we can feel safe enough to let our feelings surface. Instead of isolating ourselves, our emotions become a way to connect.

The Field of Care practice teaches us, from the very beginning, to focus on the quality of warmth and love, a fundamental aspect of field awareness that permeates everything. As we embody this warmth and it becomes part of our natural way of existing in the world, it will grow stronger and stronger as we embody ultimate awareness itself. *(On a Personal Note: see below)*[7]

Over time, we become a Field of Care for others and our spiritually homesick world. The Field of Care forms the foundation for the entire journey; in contemplative philosophy, it is called "the path of the awakened heart," which emphasizes that our core purpose comes from helping others thrive and be free. As we support others, we gain courage and strength, making our empathy even more powerful.

In Chapter 9, I will systematically introduce John Makransky's method for engaging with the Field of Care when dealing with painful emotions. Then, I will guide you through the practice of experiencing the caring qualities at the heart of our awareness as a nurturing and healing space for what feels uncomfortable, painful, or frightening. This helps us build internal space and the motivation to include more beings in our care. As we open ourselves to others' feelings, we foster a sense of belonging and solidarity with them. Emotionally, we move into a safer, more secure world.

However, before we explore this in Chapter 9, it is helpful to learn to recognize and rest in the spacious, vast, limitless, and boundless nature of awareness. This is the core of feeling at home. When we take time to notice the awake awareness that is already present, we learn to trust its existence and constant availability. The spacious, effortless, knowing quality of Loving Awareness gives us confidence in its presence, allowing us to experience ease, effortlessness, well-being, and wisdom. This confidence energizes and motivates us to stay committed to this path. The loving, compassionate side of awareness provides us with what we need to do good—for ourselves, for others, and for our world.

Compassion, as introduced by the Field of Care meditations, and wisdom, cultivated through the Loving Awareness practices, both

---

[7] ***On a Personal Note:*** *This feeling of warmth as an important quality of awareness was especially important for me, as I had experienced life in post-war Germany as harsh and frosty. The show of warmth and sensitivity in such a war-traumatized country was not supported. I remember feeling constantly physically cold as a child. The Field of Care was a live-altering and delightful discovery for me.*

provide us with the mental, emotional, and spiritual safety needed for awakening. Then, we heal our wounds and become capable of serving as a Field of Care and guiding others. While all practices promote both wisdom and compassion, they emphasize them to different degrees. Together, these practices create a comprehensive toolkit that supports us through any challenges that arise.

The Field of Care is our foundation, the stable base from which we can explore deeper awareness. But how can we systematically access the vast sky of awareness itself? This is where I call for a GPS—reliable Pointing-Out Instructions that guide us back to our true nature, no matter how lost we feel in the storms of daily life.

In Everyday Life

As you practice, notice which approaches help your heart open. Consider recording your memories of caring moments in your life. Reflect on your current emotional state and identify what would benefit you the most.

When the news cycle feels overwhelming, when anxiety about climate change arises, when you experience distrust in politicians in power, and you don't know who to trust anymore, or when political tensions escalate, remember that you can access this Field of Care. With just a few deep breaths, you can reconnect with a broader perspective that includes both your personal pain and your concerns for the world—and your own spiritual homesickness.

Many people find it helpful to set specific times during the day for practice, such as in the morning before checking the news or social media, during lunch breaks, or when transitioning from work to home. Others remember the Field of Care practice when they notice they are becoming reactive or anxious, especially when scrolling through social media or watching the news.

Instead of avoiding suffering, this practice helps you stay present with it without becoming overwhelmed or burned out.

Why This Matters Now

In times of war, political strife, and social violence, we need reliable access to something deeper than our reactive patterns. The Field of Care practice provides a crucial foundation for our spiritual journey, especially in this troubled era when many of us feel disconnected and alone, suffering from collective spiritual homesickness.

When we learn to recognize the innate care within awareness, we uncover resources we didn't realize we had. We experience natural compassion that arises not from obligation but from directly feeling the warmth that is the very essence of awareness itself. This journey isn't about escaping our spiritually homesick world but about engaging with it more fully and wisely.

As we learn to navigate between personal reality—our daily experience—and universal reality—boundless Loving Awareness—we can ultimately hold both perspectives at the same time. This integrated view helps us engage with life clearly and compassionately, even during the significant challenges of our times—bringing healing energy to our collectively longing spiritual world. *(On a Personal Note: see below)*[8]

The Field of Care forms our foundation, a secure base from which we can explore deeper levels of awareness. But how can we systematically access the vast expanse of Loving Awareness itself? This is where we need our GPS—reliable Pointing-Out Instructions that guide us back to our true nature, no matter how lost we might feel in the storms of daily life in our spiritually homesick world.

---

[8] ***On a Personal Note:*** *When I listen to my daily podcasts with their unrelenting bad news, I do not despair anymore. Now the difficult news appears as phenomena arising in this field of awareness and vanishing again. I feel the pain for myself and others, but it no longer makes me despair. It helps to stay kind and generous towards others. Engagement, in turn, gives me energy and courage.*

CHAPTER 3

The GPS Home

The Field of Care is our foundation, a secure base from which we can explore deeper levels of awareness. But how do we systematically access the vast sky of awareness itself while also recognizing our fundamental interconnectedness and discovering our authentic purpose? This is where we need a GPS—reliable Pointing-Out Instructions that can guide us home to our true nature, healing all three aspects of spiritual homesickness simultaneously.

This practice offers healing for spiritual homesickness through the systematic recognition of the triple medicine: connecting with the wisdom and warmth of the ground of being (the inexhaustible source), establishing our home there, which enables us to acknowledge fundamental interconnectedness (ending isolation), and discovering natural compassion (the foundation for meaningful service). The five progressive recognitions address all three aspects of spiritual homesickness: developing focus (calming scattered attention), recognizing emptiness (dissolving the estrangement of the separate self), accessing non-dual awareness (touching the ground of being), resting as awareness (acknowledging interconnectedness), and cultivating heart awareness (discovering natural compassion that leads to engaged service).

Min Aung sat cross-legged on a simple cushion in his cramped apartment, struggling to focus on his breath. Since arriving at the university on a student visa six months ago, he had been trying to keep up with the demanding meditation routine he learned in the monasteries back home in Myanmar. Yet, tonight, like most nights, his mind raced with worries.

His phone buzzed again—another message from his sister in Yangon. The political situation was worsening, and their neighborhood had seen more raids. His parents were safe, but their neighbor had been detained. Min squeezed his eyes tighter and tried to focus, but the knot in his stomach only grew.

Min was experiencing a double homesickness—longing for his homeland geographically while also suffering from the spiritual homesickness that affects many in our disconnected modern world. The practices that had sustained him in Myanmar's monasteries felt insufficient for dealing with his new reality of academic pressure, visa uncertainty, and being far from everything familiar.

Amid his engineering coursework, part-time campus job, and ongoing worry about his family and visa status, Min found that the traditional hour-long sitting meditations he practiced in Myanmar were becoming harder to keep up. Even more troubling, they seemed to create a split in his life—the peaceful meditator versus the worried student and son.

"I need something different," he told his academic advisor, Professor Chen, who had noticed his exhaustion. "The meditation I learned back home requires long retreats and extended sitting periods. But I can't disconnect from my responsibilities here or from what's happening at home."

Professor Chen smiled gently. "I know someone you might want to meet. She teaches a modern approach to meditation rooted in ancient contemplative traditions, but customized for busy modern lives—especially helpful for those feeling spiritual homesickness."

The following week, Min found himself at a community center where I was conducting a workshop on "Glimpse Practices"—brief moments of touching into awareness throughout the day, especially designed for those feeling spiritually homesick in our modern world.

These practices don't ask you to step away from life," I explained to the diverse group gathered there. "They invite you to recognize the clear sky of awareness that's already here, even in the midst of storm clouds. They offer a way home from spiritual homesickness that doesn't require abandoning your responsibilities or relationships."

Min was initially skeptical, but he tried the simple practice I showed them.

"Notice you're having thoughts," I instructed. "Now ask: Who or what is aware of these thoughts? Feel the space of awareness that notices the thoughts. Rest in this noticing for a breath or two."

To his surprise, Min felt a sudden shift—a broad opening right in the middle of his worry. It wasn't that his concerns about his family or his future had gone away, but they no longer took up all his attention. There was space to breathe. He had found a moment of relief from spiritual homesickness.

Over the following weeks, Min incorporated these brief "glimpses" into his daily routine. While waiting for the bus, he learned to detach awareness from his thinking mind. Between classes, he paused for thirty seconds to connect with the awareness behind his thoughts. Even when reading troubling news from home, he could briefly access the field of Loving Awareness that contained both his concern and his resolve to help.

"I'm no longer separating my spiritual life from my active life," he told Professor Chen one day. "These practices help me stay present with difficult emotions without getting overwhelmed. I can hold my worries for my family in a larger space, and this actually helps me think more clearly about how to support them."

What surprised Min the most was how these brief moments of awareness throughout his day gradually changed his relationship with everything. The background anxiety about his visa status remained a real concern, but it no longer controlled his experience. He was able to rest in a deeper sense of being while taking practical steps to secure his situation—finding refuge from spiritual homesickness without neglecting his worldly responsibilities.

"The suffering is still there," he reflected one evening. "Both my personal worries and the greater suffering in my country. But now I can face it from a place of spacious awareness rather than from contracted fear. From this space, I can respond with compassion and clarity."

As Min became more comfortable with these "Glimpse Practices," he started seeking a deeper sense of stability in his experiences. I observed his dedication and recommended Daniel P. Brown's teachings in his book *Pointing Out the Great Way.* I modified and taught those practices to a small group of committed students.

"These practices offer a systematic approach to recognizing and stabilizing awareness," I explained. "They can help you move from brief glimpses to sustained recognition—a deeper healing of spiritual homesickness."

Over the following months, Min dedicated himself to these more structured practices during evenings and weekends. My adapted Dan Brown instructions helped him to systematically recognize and rest in awareness with increasing stability. What started as fleeting moments of spaciousness gradually grew into a continuous flow that supported his daily experience.

"It's like I've found a deeper ground beneath all the turbulence," Min told his professor a year later. "The political situation at home hasn't improved, and my visa worries are still real, but something fundamental has shifted in how I see it all."

This new relationship with awareness didn't pull Min away from engagement—quite the opposite. He formed a student group supporting democracy in Myanmar and created an online platform connecting Burmese students worldwide. The depth of his practice gave him resilience and an open heart that sustained his work even in the face of discouraging news. He had found a way to ease his spiritual homesickness that actually strengthened his ability to serve.

He reported, "In a strange way, this crisis that initially threatened to overwhelm me has become the door to a much deeper spiritual life than I might have discovered otherwise. I'm not just enduring these challenges—I'm learning how to stay open-hearted and engaged because of them."

Over time, Min developed his own rhythm of practice. Walking between classes, he would pause for 30 seconds to notice awareness behind his thoughts. Before checking news from Myanmar, he would "unhook awareness from thinking mind," creating space around his concern rather than being consumed by it. These were not escapes from reality but ways of engaging more skillfully with difficult truths—ways of healing spiritual homesickness while remaining fully engaged.

"The most surprising thing," Min reflected six months later, "is that these brief moments of recognizing awareness throughout my day have become more transformative than the week-long sitting sessions I used to do. I can carry this with me everywhere, in the library, during exams, even in the middle of difficult conversations about home."

As we mend our own spiritual homesickness through these practices, we naturally become a source of healing for others experiencing the same collective disconnection. Min's transformation allowed him to serve his fellow students and his homeland from a place of sustainable compassion rather than reactive overwhelm.

The Path Home from Spiritual Homesickness

We become acquainted with the feeling of depth when experiencing the ground of being, the sacred, which allows us to access the Field of Care. When we begin to embody this field quality of awareness, we see "the clear sky behind the clouds." Through this, we experience a sense of wellness, goodness, and feeling at home—a direct antidote to spiritual homesickness. We can also feel the warmth that is a quality of this depth, allowing us to engage with our spiritually homesick world with great compassion.

I've introduced John Makransky's practice of engaging with depth through body, breath, and Loving Awareness. Now, I want to share "Pointing-out Instructions" adapted from Daniel P. Brown's teachings and Loch Kelly's "Glimpse" practices. John Makransky's, Dan Brown's, and Loch Kelly's practices come from contemplative traditions. I must note that I am not a religious scholar, but rather a serious and lifelong student. Those teachers' practices originate from systematic teachings, which are taught step-by-step, methodically, and precisely. These traditions hold that we are already awake, and our task is to remember to realize this, allowing ourselves to rest in that wakefulness.

Pointing-out Instructions are the most detailed, systematic practices that help us recognize and experience Loving Awareness step by step—like a GPS guiding us home from spiritual homesickness. Glimpse practices allow us to experience brief moments of Loving

Awareness. In his book *Effortless Mindfulness,* Loch writes, "A glimpse is not an insight from our conceptual mind; it is the direct experience of the essential peace, love, and wisdom that's always been here. It is a paradigm shift, an identity shift, a shift of consciousness to a new view and a new you that feels true."

The Road Map: Five Signposts Home from Spiritual Homesickness

The following descriptions, outlined by Daniel P. Brown, illustrate the steps on the path to experiencing Loving Awareness with greater clarity and intensity—five signposts on the journey home from spiritual homesickness. While words may have limitations, these descriptions can help you recognize your position in your practice.

The path isn't entirely straight; we might move back and forth between stages. Sometimes, we reach a certain level only to fall back to a previous one under stress. Other times, we unexpectedly experience what could be called an advanced stage. While consistent practice is important, there's also an element of surprise.

About "holding the view"

Each step in Pointing-Out Instructions is tied to a specific internal perspective or view. Holding these views requires steadiness, awareness, relaxation, and an open heart. Think about how your eye adjusts to focus on an object—your awareness similarly adjusts to see more clearly. It's said that "the view is the meditation," meaning that holding a view properly allows a particular experience of Loving Awareness to emerge effortlessly. As our view deepens, we see with "the eyes of the heart," perceiving our world as sacred and full of love. Then wisdom and compassion flow together.

Preliminary Step

Daniel P. Brown suggested starting the journey by connecting to the heart. Traditionally, people achieved this through devotion, such as connecting with a lineage of teachers. The Field of Care practice is a secular yet sacred way to open your heart—especially effective for healing spiritual homesickness.

1. Concentration and Subtle Mind: The Mountain Stream

This practice heals spiritual homesickness by uniting scattered attention—especially helpful for those experiencing mental fragmentation that often accompanies spiritual displacement.

Think of your attention as a mountain stream—initially split into many small rivulets, rushing over rocks and changing course with every obstacle. With practice in concentration, these scattered streams gradually merge into one strong flow. As you go deeper, Loving Awareness becomes like the deepest current in a river that flows steadily without stopping. When we connect with this endless stream, a feeling of home is immediately there.

The first step involves sensing the felt impressions of our bodies, which calms the mind and heart and brings us into the present moment. As we develop concentration, our minds become more flexible and ready for deeper work. Through concentration, we access a flow state and a more subtle level of consciousness.

As meditators, we often first experience this different reality in fleeting moments. This perspective has qualities of spaciousness, fluidity, lucidity, immediacy, and "now-ness." *(On a Personal Note: see below)*[9]

---

[9] ***On a Personal Note:*** *In ordinary mindfulness practice, I had been used to diligently observing my thoughts, feelings, and sensations in a methodical and microscopic way. The experience of focusing intensely, rather than witnessing slowly and carefully, brought me to a completely different place. Now I was able to reach much more swiftly beneath my conceptual mind, and the field quality of awareness began to open. Suddenly, I was in a qualitatively different state of being, which gave me a sense of surprise and awe.*

Real-life application: Building focus for real-life effectiveness

Concentration practice helps to gather a scattered mind—especially useful for those experiencing mental fragmentation, often linked to spiritual homesickness. A fragmented mind keeps us bobbing on the surface of the water, missing the depth that is always there. Many find these practices also beneficial in their daily tasks, whether it's studying, being effective at work, or managing a household. A focused mind can shift from tasks to depth. If we want to access Loving Awareness, developing some level of focus is essential.

2. Realizing Emptiness: The Cloud That Dissolves

This practice heals spiritual homesickness by dissolving rigid self-concepts that cause false separation, especially focusing on fixed ideas about what we "should" be or what life "should" provide.

Imagine building a detailed sandcastle on the beach. It looks solid and real—until a wave comes and reveals it was just sand arranged in a pattern all along. Similarly, emptiness practices help us see that what we think is solid and fixed, including our self-image, is actually fluid, constantly changing, and ultimately insubstantial.

Another metaphor could be a breeze in the sky that fades into the air or a wave that dissolves back into the ocean.

Through emptiness practices, we learn to see ourselves and the world as constructs of our own minds, essentially lacking substance. Where we once perceived solid versions of ourselves and the world, we now recognize deep fluidity and openness. This insight allows us to move into the expansive ground that has always been there, though it is so subtle that we may have missed it. Instead of getting hooked by "as if" tokens of false security, our longing for home can now rest in the groundless ground of being.

As we recognize the vastness of awareness, we see that it is filled with clarity, immediacy, a sense of knowing, an innate warmth, and "now-ness." *(On a Personal Note: see below)*[10]

Real-life application: Freedom from rigid self-concepts

When you're caught in a cycle of self-criticism or rigid beliefs about yourself—like "I always mess up" or "I'm not good enough"—practicing emptiness helps you see that these stories aren't fixed truths but flexible mental ideas that can be let go. This approach is especially healing for spiritual homesickness, which happens when we're caught up in strict ideas about what we "should" be or what life "should" offer.

3. Crossing Into Non-dual Awareness: The Swimmer Who Becomes the Ocean

This practice offers healing for spiritual homesickness by revealing our true nature as limitless Loving Awareness—the very home we've been searching for.

Imagine learning to swim by holding onto the edge of a pool. At first, letting go feels scary. But once you release your grip and float, you realize that the water has been supporting you all along. Likewise, entering non-dual awareness involves letting go of our individual perspective and recognizing that we are already immersed in a larger, all-encompassing awareness.

As we learn to access the limitless field of awareness, we begin to experience our breath, body sensations, thoughts, feelings, and

---

[10] ***On a Personal Note:*** *Emptiness practices continue to be particularly helpful to me. Especially when I get hooked in a painful self-image, like worrying that I am a "bad mother," "not-appreciated teacher," "useless author." Then, doing an emptiness-of-self practice allows me to experience the insubstantiality of a calcified self-image. I realize that these identifications are made-up, constructed, and therefore not as dense, heavy, or sticky as they first seem. I also see the relief that comes to my clients and students with emptiness practices. They feel lighter and can participate in a more spacious way of being.*

the world around us from that space. The view we have of our world slowly shifts from the personal self to field awareness.

We're exploring the non-dual nature of reality—ocean and waves are no longer seen as separate; they are both water. We begin to access the qualities of the field of awareness: wisdom, compassion, spaciousness, and well-being. We've become water, witnessing ourselves as the ocean and waves emerging and disappearing again. As we become one with the ocean and the waves, our minds let go of control, and our hearts open. *(On a Personal Note: see below)*[11]

Real-life application: Responding from wisdom rather than reactivity

When you feel overwhelmed by climate news or political division in our spiritually homesick world, practicing a state of non-dual awareness helps you respond with greater wisdom and resilience, instead of reacting with fear or reactivity. Rather than feeling paralyzed or hateful, you may discover a spaciousness, and with that, compassion and concern for those who are suffering.

4. Resting in Awareness as Awareness: The Sky and Its Weather

This practice heals spiritual homesickness by providing a steady experience that isn't dependent on external circumstances—our true home that we can never lose.

Just as the sky remains vast and unchanging regardless of the clouds, rain, or sunshine passing through it, Loving Awareness stays

---

[11] ***On a Personal Note:*** *This morning I woke up with a great sense of unease, similar to what Aaron experienced frequently in the early morning hours. The pain of the world was sitting heavy on my heart—images of wars leaving children and their families maimed, traumatized, and hungry haunted me. I felt a deep longing for the Field of Care, a sense of warmth and wisdom that is underneath this sea of suffering. Meditating, I could connect with this wider aspect of reality. Feeling held in warmth and knowing allowed me to feel rooted in a deeper ground. With deeper resilience, I could face the day and stay present and kind.*

open and clear no matter the thoughts, emotions, or experiences that arise within it.

We can now rest in the ground of being, in Big Mind, in the groundless ground of universal reality. We experience non-locality and non-duality. We see how phenomena—including ourselves, thoughts, and feelings—are dynamic, alive, and constantly changing aspects of this groundless ground.

The view here is awareness perceiving itself as both the ground and the vibrant aspects. There is limitless boundlessness, timelessness, and luminosity. Phenomena appear automatically as insubstantial or "empty." Freedom arises as we relate to our world from a wise, kind, and spacious place. Our experience of Loving Awareness gradually becomes more stable, and our homesickness subsides. *(On a Personal Note: see below)*[12]

Real-life application: Maintaining peace despite external turbulence

When facing personal challenges like illness or relationship problems, resting in Loving Awareness helps us maintain inner peace despite external chaos, placing these struggles within a broader perspective. Cultivating stable, Loving Awareness is a gradual process

---

[12] ***On a Personal Note:*** *Over the years of immersing myself in non-dual practices, the experience of Loving Awareness and a Field of Care have become more stable. My perspective has gradually shifted. I have to say, this made me a much happier person who also feels a caring equanimity. I practice staying connected with the view of awareness in the moments of change, of waking up, leaving the house, and transitioning from one situation to another. It takes practice, but it's so worth it.*

This was especially useful when I had a serious neck operation last year. I practiced during the night in the hospital and during my recovery. Resting in "the deeper ground" gave me a perspective that was invaluable. I have been teaching these practices now for a number of years. Some of my students come regularly to our online morning practice, to day-long retreats, and our teaching meditation group. I can see the slow but steady change in people, and how this wider experience is becoming part of their way of being.

that requires time, patience, and self-kindness—but it offers deep healing for spiritual homesickness.

5. Heart Awareness: The Sun That Shines Equally

This practice offers healing for spiritual homesickness by uncovering our innate compassion as the foundation for meaningful service—completing the triple medicine with genuine purpose.

Just as the sun shines its warmth equally on everything without preference, heart awareness radiates care to all beings without discrimination. The barriers between self and others melt away into a loving presence.

Understanding that awareness and all phenomena co-arise—that ocean and waves are one—we can adopt the view of simply allowing what happens to unfold naturally. We recognize that aware space and phenomena, including ourselves, are part of a single unified field of being. Our habitual patterns of grasping and pushing away fade away. This is the practice of non-doing meditation. Everything reflects the qualities of Loving Awareness: spaciousness, boundlessness, clarity, understanding, and love.

As our sense of self diminishes and our desire for control decreases, we embrace the world's sacredness with open hearts. Now, the world, seen as interconnected, unified, and sacred, becomes our home. *(On a Personal Note: see below)*[13]

---

[13] ***On a Personal Note:*** *For me, this is the fruition of practice: when I feel a sense of love and care as an underlying mood. Then there is a sense of lightness of being, and the trees, the animals, and the sky just seem beautiful. I still get dragged under when someone criticizes me, or when I witness injustice. Recently, a student client of mine texted me, very scared, as ICE was knocking on her neighbor's door. What should she do? she asked. I became very angry and fantasized about yelling at the officers. I lost the wider view completely in that moment. I was able to help this young girl, but it took me hours of walking and meditating to reach underneath the rage I was experiencing. I realize that I am better with engaging when I rest in caring equanimity. Then I am more effective as well.*

Real-life application: Authentic compassion that flows naturally

When you witness suffering in others—whether it's a homeless person on your street or victims of distant conflicts—heart awareness helps you stay open and compassionate without becoming overwhelmed. You can act from love instead of guilt or fear, offering a healing presence to our spiritually longing world.

Simple Practices to Glimpse the Sky Behind the Clouds

Practice: Background Awareness

Time needed: 10-30 seconds Glimpse

Purpose of practice: Loch Kelly's Glimpses allows us to recognize awake awareness as something we can experience directly. This practice provides healing for spiritual homesickness by connecting us with the steady ground of being that is always present

Right now:

- Take one slow, deep breath
- Let out a sigh
- Now, let your awareness open to discover the background awareness that is already effortlessly awake and aware without your help

Notice that you can effortlessly experience this background

Daily life use: Use this anytime, like when waiting in line, before meetings, or during transitions—especially helpful when spiritual homesickness feels overwhelming

Practice: Shifting Into Awareness Itself

(adapted from Loch Kelly)

Time needed: 1-2 minute Glimpse

Purpose of practice: There is a simple practice with which we learn to untangle thinking from local awake awareness

- First, we are asked to turn our awareness to the part of mind from where we perceive an object. We turn our awareness around and see where it originates from. From turning to objects, we turn to awareness itself.
- Second, we are asked to "unhook" or disidentify from the thinking mind by moving unhooked local awareness to different places in the body (to unhook means to unfasten from what is held by a hook). For example, local awareness may now be located in the jaw. Awareness and felt sense of jaw are now one, yet the thinking function is left behind.
- Third, local awake awareness might next move into the chest area, where the heart is. We feel the resonance of heart fully, as if from the inside out, yet apart from the thinking function.
- Then, local awake awareness moves behind the heart, and then further, behind the body. When Awake Awareness wraps around us, it becomes non-local, and is now called spacious Awake Awareness.

Reflection: Feel this practice in your body, heart, and mind

Key insight: Awareness isn't confined to your mind but exists everywhere. *(On a Personal Note: see below)*[14]

---

[14] ***On a Personal Note:*** *Especially during the day, I like the "unhooking" practice, as it is so simple, so clear. For me, it became a new habitual pathway like shifting gears in a car. As I feel my whole body all at once, awareness shifts away from my thinking mind, and a wider view is automatically there.*

Practice: Entering Awareness Through Memory Door

(adapted from Loch Kelly)

Time needed: 2-minute Glimpse

Purpose of practice: Access Loving Awareness through peak experience memories—healing

Entering the field quality of awareness through memory

- Settle into the sensations of your body, solid like a mountain, yet alert and relaxed
- Be aware of your entire body and ground yourself in the sensations and movement of your breath
- Remember a time when you had an extraordinary experience, an experience when you felt a sense of timelessness, presence, clarity, calm, and when you experienced reality as somehow slightly different
- Remember the environment, what the light was like, the space around you, maybe the colors and feeling tone
- Describe this experience to yourself with as many particulars as possible, but don't worry if you remember only a vague impression
- Let yourself enter into the quality of this experience, as if you were there right now—maybe a mood arises, something shifts slightly, maybe you feel your heart
- If you are tempted to go to your thoughts about this, drop those and return to bodily feeling
- Let yourself hover in the felt sense of this experience for a little while

Reflection: Feel this practice in your body, heart, and mind

Integration: This practice helps you realize that Loving Awareness has influenced your life before, giving glimpses of home even during times of spiritual homesickness. *(On a Personal Note: see below)*[15]

Key Insight: Glimpse practices are not about producing special states, but about recognizing the awareness that is always present.

Practicing In Everyday Life

These practices are not limited to your meditation cushion—they can transform how you face daily challenges in our spiritually homesick world.

Digital Overwhelm: When overwhelmed by notifications and information, the "Shiftng Into Awareness Itself" glimpse can help you step back from the digital stream and reconnect with body, local body awareness, or with spacious awareness.

Climate Anxiety: When overwhelmed by environmental news, "Awareness of Awareness Itself" helps you keep a broader perspective on these concerns. You can keep your heart open while taking wise actions instead of falling into panic or despair.

Political Polarization: When caught in us-versus-them thinking, "Extending Care" practices help you move beyond conceptual divisions and recognize our shared humanity.

Work Stress: When encountering difficult coworkers, "Entering Awareness through Memory Door" helps you respond with wisdom rather than react emotionally.

---

15 ***On a Personal Note:*** *I often go back to the memory of being about four years old, lying in a meadow. There were flowers all around. There was sun, the sounds of leaves and insects, and warmth. Time had stopped. I felt completely blissful.*

Spiritual Homesickness: When that deep longing and sense of disconnection appear, these practices offer direct routes back to your true self.

In the chapters ahead, we'll learn how to creatively use these valuable practices to face life's challenges. The stones we throw into the pond of life will create ripples that extend farther than we could ever imagine. (*On a Personal Note: see below)*[16]

Relevance for Us and Our World Now

In today's fast-changing world, these signs of Loving Awareness offer more than just spiritual comfort; they provide practical ways to build resilience and engagement for those experiencing spiritual homesickness. When we learn to shift our perception beyond our usual thinking patterns, we discover something remarkable: the heart naturally awakens as well. A sense of fundamental goodness and interconnectedness arises not as an obligation but as the most natural expression of our true nature.

Min's story illustrates that these glimpses of awareness aren't about avoiding reality but about engaging with it more fully, blending wisdom with heart-centered compassion. The desire to serve no longer feels like a burden or something we must force; instead, it naturally arises from this wellspring of awareness, like water flowing freely from an underground spring.

Whether you're dealing with workplace stress, family conflicts, existential concerns about our planet's future, or just the scattered attention of our digital age, these practices help you see the clear sky behind the clouds—a spacious, Loving Awareness that doesn't depend on perfect circumstances.

---

[16] ***On a Personal Note:*** *I use all these practices when they intuitively seem like the right fit. "Extending Care," though, is especially helpful for me when I feel political and environment rage. Rage does not allow me to act; it just makes me contract and get depressed. When I find my way into "Extending Care," then I can be engaged and effective from a place of kindness and love for others in distress.*

As you incorporate these small moments into your day, you'll find yourself navigating life's complexities with more ease, wisdom, and an open heart. You'll be able to respond instead of react, care without burning out, and stay present and compassionate, even when you're feeling spiritually homesick.

Often, the world can feel overwhelming. The path to awakened awareness changes how you live each moment, breath by breath, as your heart realizes its true nature as a gateway to inner freedom and authentic service to our troubled world.

Having glimpsed the territory of Loving Awareness through Pointing-Out Instructions, we now need to develop the ability to enter and stay in this state. This requires training our attention, not to control or manipulate awareness, but to become stable enough to recognize and rest in what is always already there—our true home beyond spiritual homesickness.

PART II

THE TRIPLE RECOGNITION—THE GROUND, INTERCONNECTION, AND PURPOSE

QR code for the audio mediations for Part II

or visit https://www.radhuleweiningerphd.com/spiritual-homesick-ness-part-two

CHAPTER 4

Concentration—Accessing the Inexhaustible Ground

As Min found, brief glimpses of awareness can change our daily lives, but many wonder: How can I build the stability to stay in this awareness more often? This is when concentration practice becomes our helper, not to force the mind into submission, but to gather our scattered attention so we can notice what has always been here—the first part of the triple medicine that provides more deep healing for spiritual homesickness.

This practice offers healing from spiritual homesickness by reconnecting us with the inexhaustible source of energy and well-being that lies within our deepest nature. Concentration helps gather the scattered mind—especially useful for those experiencing the mental fragmentation that characterizes spiritual displacement—and builds a foundation for sustained engagement without burnout.

Sarah's Story: From Scattered to Steady

Sarah, a pediatric nurse working in a busy children's hospital, described her mind as "like popcorn kernels constantly popping in a hot pan." Between twelve-hour shifts, updating patient charts, and managing her own two teenagers at home, she rarely felt present for any single moment. Even during her lunch breaks, her attention jumped between worrying about her patients, planning dinner, and scrolling through her phone.

Like many in our spiritually homesick world, Sarah felt fragmented—present in body but absent in spirit, going through the motions of a meaningful life while feeling disconnected from any more profound sense of purpose or peace.

"I keep hearing about meditation and mindfulness," she told me during a workshop at the hospital, "but whenever I try to sit quietly, my mind goes completely wild. It's like trying to calm a room full of caffeinated toddlers."

Sarah's experience reflects what many of us encounter when first engaging with contemplative practices. Our minds, conditioned by constant stimulation and multitasking, resist the urge to settle down. This resistance isn't a personal flaw; it's a natural outcome of living in a culture that fragments our attention and disconnects us from our deeper self—leading to widespread feelings of groundlessness and spiritual homesickness.

I introduced Sarah to a simple concentration practice. Allowing her awareness to fill her whole body all at once and resting in this entire field of feeling, Sarah felt calmer instantly. Then I asked her to attend to the sensation of the natural rising and falling of her breath, and then to rest in her body: "Inbreath, outbreath, body as a whole." "Think of your attention as a puppy," I suggested. "When it wanders off, you don't scold it. You gently lead it back to the natural sensation of body and breath."

At first, Sarah could barely hold her attention for three cycles before her mind jumped to her next patient or her son's upcoming soccer game. But I encouraged her to see each return to body and breath not as a failure but as a win—a moment of acknowledging where her attention had wandered and choosing to bring it back.

"The wandering isn't the problem," I explained. "The wandering is your mind doing what minds do. The practice is in the feeling and the returning."

Within a few weeks of daily practice—just ten minutes in the hospital chapel before her shifts—Sarah started to see changes. "It's like my awareness is developing more power to experience and to stay focused," she reported. "When I'm with patients now, I can actually be present instead of thinking about ten other things."

But the real change occurred during a tough shift. Sarah was caring for a seven-year-old who had been in a car accident. The child was frightened and in pain, and the parents were distressed. In previous cases like this, Sarah had felt overwhelmed by the emotional intensity, either becoming overly anxious herself or shutting down emotionally to cope.

This time, she settled into a deeper state of presence. Her breathing became steady, her mind cleared, and her heart opened to hold the family's suffering without being overwhelmed. She was able to provide not just medical care but a presence that seemed to calm everyone in the room.

Sarah reflected later, "It wasn't that I was trying to meditate. It's like the concentration practice had built a foundation of stability that existed when I needed it. I could be present with their pain without losing myself in it."

This stability gave Sarah access to what she called "a deeper knowing"—an intuitive wisdom that guided her responses. She found herself speaking to the child in just the right tone, positioning herself in ways that felt most comforting to the family, and coordinating with the medical team with remarkable clarity and efficiency.

"I realized I wasn't just helping them medically," she said. "I was creating a peaceful space amid chaos. My calm presence was becoming healing medicine for their fear—and for my own sense of spiritual longing."

Over the following months, Sarah's concentration practice deepened. She shifted from ten-minute sessions to twenty-minute periods, and sometimes longer periods, on her days off. She noticed that the steadiness she gained during formal practice began to influence her entire day.

"My teenagers even remarked that I seem less stressed," she laughed during a follow-up conversation. "I can listen to their problems without immediately jumping into fix-it mode. There's space around everything now."

But perhaps most notably, Sarah began to experience what she called "moments of pure presence"—brief moments when her usual sense of being a separate, stressed individual faded into something much larger.

"During one meditation session, I lost track of where I ended and the rest of the world began," she described. "It wasn't scary—it was like coming home to something I'd been missing without even realizing it. The loneliness I didn't even know I was carrying just melted away."

These experiences of expanded awareness didn't occur every time she meditated, but they became more common. More importantly, the stability she was developing through concentration practice allowed her to recognize and rest in these insights when they appeared—healing her spiritual homesickness by directly acknowledging her true nature.

"I'm starting to realize that concentration isn't about forcing my mind to be silent," Sarah reflected. "It's about cultivating enough steadiness to recognize the awareness that's already present, even when my thoughts are active. That awareness feels like the most natural and peaceful thing in the world."

As we work on healing our own spiritual homesickness through concentration practice, we naturally become more available to serve others. Sarah's transformation allowed her to offer a healing presence to patients and families experiencing their own forms of spiritual displacement and alienation during medical crises.

Why Focus Matters for Spiritual Freedom

Sarah's journey emphasizes a key point: practicing concentration can help us touch into Loving Awareness. And more importantly, it offers the stability to recognize and rest in the awareness that is always already present.

The ability to focus calms and stabilizes the small mind, which includes the brain's cognitive and processing functions involved in conceptualizing, ruminating, planning, scheming, worrying, or panicking. When our small mind remains untamed, it can feed depressive or anxiety-filled thoughts that spill into our lives.

Imagine your mind as a lake. When it is restless and full of waves of thoughts and emotions, it doesn't reflect clearly. But as it calms through concentration practice, it becomes a still lake that mirrors the sky and landscape perfectly. This calmness helps us see reality more clearly.

Focusing our mind offers another key benefit: it helps us develop "meta-cognitive awareness," the ability to recognize where we are in our practice and quickly self-correct when we get lost in rumination or daydreams. It's like building an inner GPS that gently guides us back on track when we stray.

In our hyperconnected, digitally fragmented world, where spiritual homesickness has become increasingly common, most of us have minds that are scattered across multiple streams of information, worry, and stimulation simultaneously. While this mental agility can be useful for multitasking, it hinders our ability to reach the deeper levels of awareness that are the source of wisdom, compassion, and genuine fulfillment.

The Three Levels of Concentration

There are different levels of concentration, each offering their own gifts.

1. Initial Concentration (Calming the Storm)

This practice provides relief from spiritual homesickness by easing scattered, anxious thoughts.

At this stage, we learn to skillfully manage our wandering attention. Like Sarah's experience with her "popcorn mind," we practice becoming aware when our focus drifts and gently guiding it back to our chosen object—often the breath. This phase is marked by:

- Frequent mind-wandering accompanied by increasing awareness of it
- Periods of calm broken by mental agitation
- Cultivating patience throughout the process
- Starting to feel moments of presence and calm *(On a Personal Note: see below)*[17]

---

[17] ***On a Personal Note:*** *When I first learned how to meditate in a monastery in the jungle of Sri Lanka in 1982, my "popcorn" mind found the first moments of relief from distraction and self-torture with this first level of meditation.*

Benefits for daily life:

- Enhanced ability to stay present in conversations
- Reduced reactivity to stressful situations
- Better sleep as the mind learns to relax
- Improved focus on tasks without frequent distractions
- Initial relief from the scattered feeling of spiritual homesickness

2. Sustained Concentration (Finding the River's Flow)

This practice helps heal spiritual homesickness by enabling access to deeper states of well-being and natural joy.

As practice continues, the mind naturally settles into states of sustained attention. Less effort is needed to stay focused, and periods of calm become longer and deeper. This stage includes:

- Extended periods of sustained focus
- Natural emergence of states of ease and well-being
- Less effort to maintain focus
- Spontaneous moments of joy or contentment during practice *(On a Personal Note: see below)*[18]

Benefits for daily life:

- Improved creativity and problem-solving skills
- Natural development of compassion and patience towards others
- Ability to stay calm in tough situations
- A deeper appreciation for simple experiences
- A growing sense of inner fullness and depth that counters spiritual homesickness

---

[18] ***On a Personal Note:*** *During these weeks in this Sri Lankan monastery, I entered the second level of concentration, which includes effortless focus. When I returned to University, medical school in fact, I was amazed how much easier it was to concentrate, even on boring subjects.*

3. Effortless Concentration (Merging With the Ocean)

This practice helps heal spiritual homesickness by offering direct access to the limitless source of energy and love.

At deeper levels, the effort to concentrate diminishes into a natural state of absorption. The meditator, the act of meditation, and the object of meditation begin to merge into a single experience. This level is characterized by:

- Maintaining attention with ease
- Dissolution of the sense of "doing" meditation
- Natural emergence of states of bliss, clarity, and peace
- Spontaneous expansion into greater awareness *(On a Personal Note: see below)*[19]

Benefits for daily life:

- Actions flow from intuitive wisdom rather than mental planning
- Natural response to what each situation calls for
- Consistent sense of well-being regardless of external circumstances
- Spontaneous emergence of love and compassion for more and more people
- Move towards healing of spiritual homesickness through direct awareness of one's true nature

Concentration as Gateway, Not Goal

It's important to realize that concentration practice, while valuable in itself, serves as a gateway to recognizing Loving Awareness rather than its final goal. As the mind becomes more stable and

---

[19] ***On a Personal Note:*** *Before, I reached these very deep levels of experience only on several-week-long silent retreats, and now, through the direct path of non-dual awareness. In these most subtle levels of awareness, I truly experienced a feel of home, of being effortlessly one with the ground of being.*

settled, we naturally start to notice the awareness within which all mental activity happens.

This awareness—spacious, knowing, and inherently peaceful—is what we mean by Loving Awareness. It's not something we create through concentration; it's what becomes apparent when the mind is settled enough to recognize what was always there—our true home beyond spiritual homesickness.

Common Obstacles and How to Work With Them

1. "My mind is too busy"

Working with it: Remember that a busy mind isn't an obstacle to practice—it's exactly why practice is beneficial. Each time you notice your mind has wandered and bring it back to your chosen focus, you're strengthening your awareness.

2. "I don't have time"

Working with it: Begin with very short periods—even five minutes can be helpful. The quality of attention matters more than the amount of time. Sarah started with ten minutes and found it changed her entire day.

3. "Nothing seems to happen"

Working with it: Concentration practice often works subtly, like physical exercise. You might not notice changes during practice, but others may comment on your increased patience or presence. Trust the process.

4. "I feel restless or agitated"

Working with it: Sometimes, concentration practice initially brings awareness of the underlying restlessness that has always been there but is masked by constant activity. This is normal and will settle with continued practice. The restlessness of spiritual homesickness often surfaces before it can be healed.

5. "I fall asleep"

Working with it: This often indicates that you need rest. As you develop the skill, you'll find a balance between relaxation and alertness. Try practicing with your eyes slightly open or in a more upright posture.

When Concentration Deepens: Opening to Loving Awareness

As concentration stabilizes, something remarkable often occurs: the effort of focusing begins to fade, and you naturally settle into a state of open, expansive awareness. This is the gateway opening to Loving Awareness.

Sarah described this transition beautifully: "It's like I was working so hard to hold onto my breath, and then I realized the breath was holding me. I could relax into something that was already supporting me all along."

This shift from effortful focus to effortless awareness represents a major change in practice. You're no longer just developing the ability for sustained attention; you're also starting to recognize the awareness where all experience happens—the true remedy for spiritual homesickness.

Building the Foundation: Progressive Focus Training

So, how can we build this essential skill of focus? Let me share some methods that have been refined over centuries and have been especially helpful for my students, who, like me, often struggle with focus.

Setting the Foundation

Before beginning formal concentration practice, think about these basic elements.

Posture matters, but comfort is key. Find a position that keeps you both alert and relaxed. Sitting upright helps maintain focus, while relaxing your shoulders, arms, and face prevents unnecessary tension. Think "dignified but comfortable"—like a mountain that is both solid and at ease.

Begin with your heart. Spending just a minute or two connecting with your heart's intention lays a solid foundation for your practice. This can be as simple as thinking of someone who loves you, feeling the earth beneath you, or offering a brief prayer or dedication that resonates with you. As I mentioned in Chapter 2, this heart connection calms the nervous system and creates fertile ground for concentration.

My student Maria begins each session by placing her hand on her heart and silently saying, "May this practice help me be more present for those I love." She believes this simple gesture fully transforms the quality of her meditation.

A Gentle Approach to Concentration

Rather than presenting the practice as a strict sequence, I will share it as a journey of exploration.

1. Settle into your body

Start by noticing the sensations in your body. Feel where your body touches the chair, cushion, or floor. Notice the weight, pressure, and temperature. Experience your body as a whole—not by analyzing or overthinking, but by directly feeling the sense of being present in your body right now. With that, awareness shifts from the thinking mind into the whole body.

When I first started practicing this way, I was surprised by how much time I spent thinking about my body instead of feeling it directly. Can you feel the difference? Thinking creates commentary: "My knee hurts a bit. I wonder if I should adjust it." Direct experience means feeling the body from the inside out. Allow yourself to be drawn into the unity of awareness and body, body and awareness.

There's a clear sense that something has shifted when awareness moves from the thinking mind to body awareness. This results in a feeling of ease and effortlessness.

2. Find your breath

From this embodied awareness, observe how your breath flows effortlessly. There's no need to control or alter it—simply feel the sensations of breathing. Notice the in-breath, the out-breath, and the brief pause between them. Be aware of how your entire body subtly moves with each breath.

I like to think of this as befriending my breath—getting to know its rhythms and textures as I would with a new friend; becoming one with it. Sometimes, the breath is deep and full; other times, it is shallow and quick. Whatever its pattern, stay with it moment by moment. Slowly, feel your breath from the inside out. Awareness and breath become one. Allow yourself to be drawn into the oneness of awareness and breath.

3. When your mind wanders, come back with kindness

Your mind will wander—that's natural! When you notice you've become lost in thoughts, memories, or planning, gently bring your focus back to the sensations of your body and breath. Do this without judgment or frustration, much like patiently guiding a puppy back to its bed.

One of my students, David, found it helpful to intensify his focus on the sensations in his body when he became distracted, while remaining relaxed. His mind settled when he returned, gently but firmly, to his intensely felt bodily sensations while staying at ease at the same time.

4. Find the balance, the sweet spot, between effort and ease

As you continue, experiment with the effort you put into your practice. Sometimes, you need to intensify your focus, feeling each breath with precision and clarity. Other times, when you hold your mind too tight, you could instead relax and let the breath flow naturally.

This is like tuning a guitar string: too tight, and it snaps; too loose, and it won't produce sound. Through trial and error, you'll find the "sweet spot" where your mind stays with the breath without effort. Then, you realize that breath sustains you.

5. Work with obstacles skillfully

Two common challenges in concentration practice are dullness, which refers to sleepiness or mental fog, and agitation, characterized by restlessness or excessive thinking.

To fight dullness, picture yourself sitting in a bright, open space filled with light. Slightly lift your gaze, straighten your posture, or take a few deep breaths. Sometimes, widening your eyes or even standing briefly can help boost alertness.

For agitation, imagine yourself sitting in a protected, dimly lit space—safe and contained. Lower your gaze, relax your breathing, and focus more on the sensations of your body touching the floor or chair, reinforcing the feeling of being grounded.

6. Notice the transition to subtle mind

With regular practice, you may begin to notice a shift in the quality of your awareness. The breath starts to feel as if it is breathing itself, beyond your control. Your sense of effort diminishes, replaced by a natural flow of attention. Colors may seem brighter and sounds clearer. There is often a sensation of lightness or even joy.

This marks the beginning of what we call "subtle mind"—a more refined level of awareness that naturally emerges as concentration deepens. When this occurs, simply rest in this awareness and allow it to stabilize and deepen.

Formal Concentration Practice

In all Pointing-Out-Style practices, it is important to set up your posture carefully at the beginning of the practice. This is especially true for concentration practices, where good posture encourages alertness and focus. After your initial dedication, keep your eyes slightly open with a relaxed, unfocused gaze at about a 40-degree angle. If you're used to eyes-closed meditation, be patient with yourself and gradually adapt to this way of practicing. *(On a Personal Note: see below)*[20]

Practice: Twelve-Step Pointing-Out Style Concentration

Time needed: 15 -20 minutes

Purpose of practice: Develop strong concentration leading to subtle mind recognition

Preparation:

1. **Set the body up for meditation**
   - Close your eyes, and let your awareness drop down into your body

---

[20] ***On a Personal Note:*** *The twelve-step pointing-out-style concentration practice surprised me by how well it worked. When I first learned this style of practice by Daniel P. Brown, I was shocked by how I suddenly could focus impeccably. Beforehand, I had struggled beforehand greatly to stay focused. I realized that deepening concentration was like driving a stick-shift car. With each gear, the driving (concentration) got smoother and more effortless. As I entered subtle mind, concentration became automatic. During that experience, the view of subtle mind supports concentration, and concentration supports the transition into subtle mind.*

- Settle yourself into the sensations in your body
- Feel the contact between body and chair, cushion, or ground
- Sit solid like a mountain, your body straight and alert, yet with your shoulders, arms, and face relaxed
- Feel your body as a whole, the felt sense of your whole body all at once

2. Set up a heart-opening practice or dedication (one possible example)

- Remember a person, animal, religious figure, or a beautiful part of the natural world
- Bring this moment of care into the present moment, right in front of you
- Feel the energy of care, of love, of support as it is here right now
- Let the memory go, and rest for a moment in that feeling; the felt sense

3. Set up an open, spacious view

- Open your eyes slightly, keeping them relaxed and unfocused
- Hold the view of light flooding through you, connecting inside with outside
- Imagine that open, seamless space is all around you
- Now mix space with awareness, and awareness with space
- Linger in this feeling of resting in aware, wide-awake space for a while

Practice: Building concentration

4. Intensify the felt sense of body

- Now, look a little closer and feel your entire body more distinctly as it experiences the felt sense of your whole body all at once
- Feel each moment, each inch, each pixel of your body as awake and alive

5. Find 3-Point Breath

- Feel the three-point breath: inbreath, outbreath, and your body as a whole
- From this entire realm of bodily sensations, feel the breath rising with the inhale, release with the exhale, and then sense the body as a whole
- Feel every moment of the inbreath, every moment of the outbreath, very clearly, until you distinctly feel this entire cycle of body and breath
- Inhale, exhale, body as a whole

6. Intensify body and breath

- Now feel body and breath more distinctly
- Intensify your attention to the whole cycle of body and breath while remaining relaxed at the same time, until each point in this cycle of breath becomes clear and lucid

Refine your practice

7. Redirect Mind Wandering

- Whenever your mind wanders and gets distracted by sounds, thoughts, daydreams, and feelings.

- Redirect your focus to your breath and body, just as you would guide a playful puppy's mind.
- Please repeatedly refocus your attention on the body and breath, no matter how often it takes.
- Every part of this breath-body cycle is clear, lucid, and focused.

8. Adjust for Drowsiness

- For a moment, notice the energy in your body
- When you start to feel drowsy or sluggish, imagine yourself in a bright, open space filled with light
- Stay there for a while
- You might notice your energy increasing, becoming clearer and more alert

9. Adjust for Agitation

- When, on the contrary, you feel agitated and distracted, picture yourself sitting in a dimly lit, secure space, enclosed and safe
- See if that helps soothe your mind and enhances your practice.

10. Intensify and ease up

- Again, notice your inhale and exhale, and how your body feels as a whole
- Increase the intensity once more, being strong yet relaxed at the same time
- Now ease up a bit and let the reins go just a little looser
- See how that feels
- When you observe that your mind is beginning to wander, refocus your attention and connect with the object of your focus
- And then ease up again

Entering the subtle mind

11. Sense the transition

- Now you might find that breath occurs on its own, automatically, without needing to manage or control it
- Feel how that resonates; truly embrace it
- You may now experience many particles of breath, like shards of energy
- Feel the breath move on its own
- Feel the space around your breath
- Feel the lightness and clarity of this breath breathing all by itself, as if breath becomes pixilated energy
- Allow yourself to surrender to your breath
- Let breath breathe you, as the quality of awareness in the field emerges naturally

12. Rest in subtle mind

- Keep your eyes slightly open and rest in the entire field of awareness around you in a relaxed yet alert way
- Focus, deepen, and relax until you can hold steadily with your breath in a continuous, automatic flow
- When you become distracted, stabilize even more
- Deepen and smooth your breath, fostering an alert yet relaxed flow
- Notice how the mind is workable and useful; focus and evenness become second nature
- Now you are resting in a deeper level of mind
- For a moment, reflect on how this practice is felt in your body, heart, and mind

Reflection: Feel this practice in your body, heart, and mind

Troubleshooting:

Too tight: Ease up

Too loose: Intensify attention while staying relaxed
Lost in thought: Gently return, no judgment needed
Energy imbalanced: Use bright/ dim space visualization

Signs of Progress:

Breath feels automatic, effortless
Sense of lightness and subtle energy in the body
Colors appear brighter, sounds clearer
Natural flow of attention without effort
Natural sense of wellbeing and ease

Taking Your Meditation on a Walk

Another way to practice besides sitting is to walk with awareness. I often take my meditation practice "on a walk," which is a wonderful, expansive, full-bodied way to experience attention leading to body awareness. Full-bodied awareness can then lead to subtle, all-around awareness. *(On a Personal Note: see below)*[21]

---

[21] *On a Personal Note: I made taking my meditation on a walk one of my main practices. Almost every afternoon, I walk in a nature preserve close to my house, overlooking the Pacific Ocean.*

I walk at about 60% of my normal speed, very steady and relaxed. My little elderly Chihuahua dog, Lucy, follows me. Sometimes my son's dog, Raul, is also there. Both are mellow. Sometimes I walk quietly, sometimes I listen to a guided meditation through my earphones. As I enter subtle mind, I realize the increased sense of ease and calm. The tree branches and leaves become luminous, and the sky seems even more clear and lucid. There is a great sense of effortlessness.

Once a year, I walk the Camino de Santiago in Spain, a pilgrimage path. The daily walking on a pre-marked path for many hours a day is super useful for such a practice. After a week or ten days of walking, I am usually in a transcended, calm, luminous, and most of all completely happy state. It's as if I love every person, every animal, every tree, and every flower on this path.

Practice: Walking With Awareness

Time needed: 10-30 minutes

Purpose: Develop concentration through mindful movement—this practice offers healing for an aching heart and spiritual homesickness by connecting awareness with embodied moving presence

Instructions:

1. Choose a path, if possible, outdoors
2. Begin walking slowly and pay attention to the physical sensations in the soles of your feet
3. Feel how your feet touch the ground, the movement of your legs
4. Feel your entire body as you walk
5. Choose a comfortable speed, 40 to 60% of your usual speed
6. Notice how awareness permeates your entire body, and your entire body is experienced as awareness
7. Keep walking slowly and mindfully, while physical sensations anchor your attention
8. When your mind wanders to thoughts or external distractions, gently refocus your attention on the sensations of your entire body, now walking as awareness
9. You might feel awareness within and around you, while also feeling the touch of your feet on the ground and your breath expanding and letting go all by itself

Reflection: Feel this practice in your body, heart, and mind

Benefits: Especially useful for those who struggle with sitting meditation or are naturally kinesthetic learners. Effective for calming the restlessness often associated with spiritual homesickness.

Integration into Daily Life

The real test of concentration practice comes in integrating it into daily activities.

Informal Practice Opportunities:

- **Waiting periods:** Use time in lines, traffic, or appointments as opportunities for brief concentration practice, letting your whole body fill with embodied awareness
- **Routine activities:** Bring full embodied attention to washing dishes, brushing teeth, or preparing meals
- **Transitions:** Take three conscious breaths, feeling with your full attention your whole body expanding and contracting when moving between activities
- **Work breaks:** Use brief periods of full body awareness rather than checking phones
- **Nature connection:** Spend a few minutes being fully aware of natural sounds, sights, or sensations

Signs of Developing Concentration

As your practice develops, you may notice:

- Increased ability to stay present during conversations
- Less mental commentary during daily activities
- Natural arising of calm states during practice
- Improved capacity to handle stress without becoming reactive
- Spontaneous moments of appreciation or gratitude
- Growing sense of inner stability that doesn't depend on external circumstances
- Healing of the scattered, disconnected feeling of spiritual homesickness

Concentration and Compassionate Engagement

Contrary to some misconceptions, developing concentration does not make us detached from the world or less attentive to others' needs. Instead, it offers the inner stability needed for wise and compassionate engagement with our spiritually homesick world.

Sarah's experience with her young patient clearly illustrates this. Her concentration practice didn't lessen her concern for her patient's suffering; instead, it provided her with the stability to stay present with that suffering without becoming overwhelmed. From this centered presence, her natural compassion could flow more freely and effectively.

This is the gift that concentration offers to our troubled world: not an escape from its challenges, but the inner resources to face those challenges with wisdom, compassion, and skillful action. Concentration allows us to drop into our own depth—the depth that has always been there. When we can stay centered amid chaos, we become a stabilizing force for others—bringing healing medicine to our spiritually homesick world. *(On a Personal Note: see below)*[22]

Building Your Personal Practice

As you build your own concentration practice, remember that consistency is more important than length. It's better to practice for

---

[22] ***On a Personal Note:*** *I experienced, when entering higher levels of practice, that challenges can become enhancements on the path. I remember a time some years ago when I was in a very painful, hurtful situation with a person I had known for a long time. Suddenly, in the middle of her attacking me, I was standing there dumbfounded. Suddenly, there was this feeling of sacredness, like a clear, warm, yet strong breeze. It was as if this breeze was enveloping me, and I could disentangle myself from this situation with peace. I was greatly surprised.*

I now remember that Joseph Goldstein described a similar situation at the beginning of his foreword to this book. This clear, peaceful, invisible energy came forward and helped to transform a crisis into a peaceful situation.

ten minutes every day than for an hour once a week. Like physical exercise, the benefits grow gradually with regular practice.

Most importantly, approach concentration practice with patience and kindness toward yourself. Like Sarah discovered, the goal isn't to achieve a perfectly calm mind but to build a stable foundation from which you can recognize the awareness that is your true nature—your true home beyond spiritual homesickness.

In the next chapter, we'll explore how this stable attention underpins the deep practice of "emptiness"—recognizing the fluid, insubstantial nature of our usual sense of self and opening into the vast space of Loving Awareness that is our true identity.

CHAPTER 5

Emptiness—Dissolving the Barriers to Interconnection

With a stronger foundation in concentration practice that enhances our attention, we're prepared to explore one of the most profound yet often misunderstood practices in contemplative traditions: recognizing the "emptiness" of our separate self. Far from being nihilistic or cold, this practice provides the most direct path to freedom from the limited sense of separation that causes spiritual homesickness.

This practice heals spiritual homesickness by dissolving rigid self-views that create a false sense of separation—particularly effective for addressing feelings of spiritual loneliness and confusion, which often arise from strict ideas about what we "should" be or what life "should" offer. The emptiness practice addresses the second part of the triple disconnection: our sense of separation from others and from life itself.

David's Journey: From Solid Self to Spacious Being

David, a 45-year-old middle school principal, attended one of my workshops carrying what he described as "the weight of everyone else's expectations on my shoulders." After twenty years in education, he had built a strong identity as someone who could handle any crisis, solve any problem, and support any struggling student or teacher.

"I know who I am," he said with a mix of pride and exhaustion. "I'm the reliable one, the person who doesn't fall apart when everything else is crumbling. But lately, this feels like a prison I've built for myself."

Like many successful people, David was experiencing a specific type of spiritual homesickness—the overwhelming burden of a rigid self-identity that, while helping him professionally, had become a barrier to experiencing the freedom and joy he had known as a child.

The weight became especially evident during the pandemic when his role expanded to support not only his school community but also managing his own family's remote learning, his aging parents' health concerns, and the overall anxiety that seemed to permeate everything.

"I feel like I'm wearing a suit of armor that I can't take off," he explained. "Even when I'm alone, I'm still being 'the principal,' still holding it all together. I don't remember the last time I felt... light."

David had tried traditional meditation but found it frustrating. "My mind just spins through all the problems I need to solve tomorrow. I can't seem to turn off the part of me that's always in charge."

I introduced David to a gentle version of what contemplative traditions call "emptiness practice"—a systematic way of exploring the nature of our sense of self. I was careful to explain that "emptiness" doesn't mean becoming vacant or losing our identity, but rather discovering the spacious, fluid nature of who we truly are beneath our fixed self-concepts.

Think of your sense of being 'David the principal,'" I suggested. "Can you feel where that identity exists in your body? Is it in your chest, your head, or your shoulders?"

David closed his eyes and scanned his body. "It's like a tightness across my chest and shoulders, and there's this constant voice in my head that's always planning and organizing."

"Now," I continued, "using your attention like a gentle flashlight, can you look for the real 'David' who's carrying all this responsibility? Not the thoughts about being responsible, but the person who supposedly has these thoughts."

David spent several minutes searching. At first, he only thought more about responsibility, felt more pressure, and saw mental images of his school and its needs. But as he kept gently exploring, something shifted.

"This is strange," he said, opening his eyes in surprise. "The more I look for this solid 'David' who's supposed to be handling everything, the less I can find him. It's like searching for someone inside a shadow."

"What do you find instead?" I asked.

"Space," he said quietly. "And a kind of... awareness that's much bigger than my usual sense of myself. It's like I've been living in a small room and suddenly discovered that the walls are just imaginary."

This was David's first experience of what contemplatives call "the emptiness of the separate self"—not a void or vacuous space, but the understanding that our usual strong sense of identity is actually a mental creation that can dissolve, revealing the spacious awareness that is our deeper nature.

Over the following weeks, David practiced this gentle inquiry every day. He would ask himself: "Who is the one having this stressful thought? Where is the David who feels overwhelmed?" He would not investigate with his "thinking mind," but instead search for the "feeling sense" of that sense of self throughout his body. Each time, the search would lead not to a fixed self but to an opening into spacious awareness.

"It's not that I stop being effective at my job," he said after a month of practice. "If anything, I'm more responsive to what each situation actually needs because I don't filter everything through preconceived ideas about what 'David the principal' should do. Then I hear the voice of my intuition more clearly."

The real transformation became clear during a particularly tough week when a student brought a weapon to school. In previous crises, David would have instantly shifted into his "crisis management mode," his body tense with responsibility, his mind racing through protocols and procedures.

This time, while still responding appropriately to ensure everyone's safety, David operated from a state of calm and openness. "It was like the crisis was happening within a much larger space," he explained. "I could respond to what was needed without feeling like I personally had to carry the weight of everyone's fear."

He coordinated with police, counseled the student's family, handled concerned parents, and supported his staff—all while resting in what he described as "a kind of easeful knowing that seemed to arise by itself."

"The strangest thing," David reflected, "is that everyone commented on how calm and capable I seemed, but from my perspective, I wasn't 'trying' to be calm. The calmness was just there when I stopped holding onto my usual tight sense of self."

Six months into his practice, David observed a fundamental shift in how he experienced daily life. "I still care deeply about my students and my work, but I no longer feel like I'm carrying it all on my shoulders. It's as if I've discovered a much larger intelligence guiding me, and my job is to stay open to that rather than trying to figure everything out with my thinking mind."

The practice had given David access to what he called "effortless effectiveness"—the ability to respond wisely and compassionately to difficult situations without feeling personally drained, as he had for decades. He discovered freedom from the prison of his rigid self-image while actually becoming better at helping others—healing his spiritual homesickness by recognizing his true nature.

As we begin to heal our own spiritual homesickness through emptiness practice, we naturally become more available to serve others. David's transformation allowed him to offer spacious presence to students and staff experiencing their own forms of spiritual displacement and overwhelm.

Ancient Insight, Still Relevant Today

Two thousand five hundred years ago, it was the Buddha who discovered that understanding the emptiness of self was the key to enlightenment while he meditated under the Bodhi tree. He realized that he and all phenomena were neither solid nor independent but instead an open, fluid, and constantly changing expression of life—what we might now call "emergent phenomena." He saw this insight as a crucial step on the path to freeing oneself from self-focus and, consequently, from suffering. Other spiritual teachers arrived at similar insights.

While practicing emptiness is essential, it's also important to understand that the goal isn't to eliminate our ego. A clear and healthy sense of self is crucial for navigating society effectively. Loch Kelly explains, "Ego-identification... doesn't have to be fought, repressed, extinguished, denied, or killed. We don't become a nobody, an angel, or a couch potato. Instead, when we discover Awake Awareness as our true nature, our ego functions can return to their natural roles." From the broad, clear, and loving perspective of awareness itself, we can relate to others and our environment with confidence and kindness.

The emptiness-of-self practice is never about destroying our personal selves. Instead, we learn to understand our ego's needs from a broader, wiser, and most importantly, compassionate perspective. For example, when we reflect on our lives, it may become clear how our selves were shaped as children within the family system we're born into. We might realize how we learned to seek love by becoming a certain type of person. We may have tried to be especially helpful to our parents, or perhaps we unconsciously became defensive and withdrawn due to a sense of danger. Recognizing this now, we can see ourselves with compassion.

Understanding Emptiness: What It Is and What It Isn't

David's experience highlights several key aspects of emptiness practice that counter common misconceptions.

What Emptiness Is Not:

- Becoming vacant, spaced-out, or disconnected from life
- Losing your personality, preferences, or unique qualities
- Becoming indifferent to others' suffering or your own well-being
- A nihilistic view that nothing matters
- Suppressing thoughts, emotions, or normal human responses

What Emptiness Is:

- Recognizing the fluid, constructed nature of our usual sense of self
- Discovering the spacious awareness that is our deeper identity
- Freedom from rigid self-concepts that lead to unnecessary suffering
- Opening to a more flexible, responsive way of being in the world
- Access to wisdom and compassion that flow from our essential nature
- Healing from the deep separation that results in spiritual homesickness

The Journey from Identity to Presence

Emptiness practice gradually shifts our sense of identity from seeing ourselves as a solid, separate person to realizing we are expressions of spacious, aware presence. This isn't achieved through force or mental manipulation, but through gentle, persistent openness to a different experience.

Stage 1: Recognizing the Constructed Self

We start by recognizing that our sense of self is really a collection of thoughts, memories, roles, and identities rather than a fixed thing.

- "I am a teacher" (role)
- "I am responsible" (personality trait)
- "I am the one who handles crises" (self-image)
- "I, as an educator, am stressed about tomorrow's meeting" (current state)

Through careful exploration, we start to see that these are mental constructs rather than our true identity.

Stage 2: The Search for the Self

Using attention like a searchlight, we seek the true "self" that supposedly holds these thoughts and experiences. This isn't an analytical process but a direct, experiential exploration.

- Who is the one thinking these thoughts?
- Where is the "I" that feels stressed?
- Can I find the one who is searching?

Typically, this search doesn't reveal a solid self but unfolds into expansive awareness, which mends the pain of spiritual homesickness. The formal emptiness practice further below will guide you step-by-step.

Stage 3: Resting in Spacious Awareness

As the solid sense of self dissolves, we don't disappear—we uncover our deeper nature as awareness itself. This awareness is:

- Spacious and boundless
- Naturally peaceful and at ease
- Inherently knowing and intelligent
- The source of wisdom and compassion
- Our true home beyond spiritual homesickness

Stage 4: Sense of Self, Fluid Like a Rainbow

As I begin to understand that identity is constructed, I also realize that a particular sense of self is still there, but now fluid, like a rainbow appearing and disappearing in the background. It is:

- Fluid and impermanent
- Insubstantial yet occurring
- Arising from awareness and dissolving back into it

Practices to Experience Emptiness-of-Separate-Self

These practices are designed to help you directly experience the emptiness of the separate self. While they work well when done in sequence, you can also use them individually as needed.

Pointing-Out: Emptiness- of-Self-Practice

Practices of emptiness-of-self open the door to Awake Awareness. These practices encourage openness to the self, thoughts, emotions, and perceptions, including sound, sight, smell, taste, touch, and body sensations.

Preparation:

For all emptiness practices, I recommend:

- Beginning with a dedication
- Maintaining a spacious view
- Using focusing practice to enter the subtle level of mind
- Allowing for trust in yourself and your practice
- Connecting with your heart space
- Keeping your eyes slightly open with a relaxed, unfocused gaze directed about forty degrees downward

Begin by settling into your body and breathing the three-point breath:

1. Concentrate, intensify, and ease up until your breath flows automatically
2. When distracted, stabilize further
3. Find an awake, relaxed flow
4. Notice how focus continues automatically, and you rest in the subtler level of mind

Practice: Emptiness-of-Self

Time needed: 15 minutes

Purpose: To realize that our sense-of-self is a construct, not solid and permanent

Preparation:

- Begin with concentration until breath flows automatically
- Maintain a spacious view with slightly open eyes
- Connect briefly with the Field of Care for emotional safety

Practice:

1. **Activate a sense of self**

    - Settle into meditation and activate your usual sense-of-self
    - Bring this sense-of-self to life (your "you-ness")
    - Create a clear image of who you feel yourself to be

2. **Search for this self systematically**

    - Undertake an honest search for this entity, you see as yourself
    - Look for anything solid, unchanging, independently existing
    - Use your high-speed awareness to search your head for your sense of self

3. **Notice unfindability**

    - The more you search, the more this sense-of-self glides away
    - Experience its unfindability

- Notice the spaciousness that emerges within and around your head

4. **Expand your search**

- Search for any solid, independently existing self in your chest, belly, heart, limbs
- Make a thorough search with your high-speed awareness
- Notice how your sense-of-self as an entity remains unfindable

5. **Rest in awareness**

- Notice what remains: openness, a field of awareness
- Recognize that while your sense-of-self feels real, it's not an independently existing "thing"
- Instead, see that the sense-of-self is still there, but no longer permanent and solid
- The insubstantial self may be there fleetingly, like a rainbow in the sky
- It's now part of a bigger, open field of awareness

6. **Final search and rest**

- Make one more search through your whole body
- Look for anything concrete or independently existing that is "you"
- Notice that there is sensation, but nothing solid is there
- Be curious about what's left: spaciousness, freshness, lightness, and warmth
- Rest in this openness and enjoy

Reflection: Feel this practice in your body, heart, and mind.

Key Insight: You haven't lost yourself; you've uncovered your true nature as awareness itself, with self-sense being just one expression rather than the center. Spiritual homesickness is gradually being healed.

Navigating the Fear That Sometimes Arises

When we think of ourselves as empty and realize that our bodies, thoughts, and feelings are not unchanging and solid, but rather fleeting phenomena, we may experience a momentary fear of "not-being." This reaction is a natural response.

When we truly understand what it is, we can show kindness and warmth to this scared little "ego child" and notice how, as we do, it relaxes in our embrace. Once the ego releases some control, it stays present but now exists within a larger space of care. A sense of relief and openness begins to emerge, as if a weight has been lifted from our shoulders.

My student Thomas shared his experience: "When I first practiced emptiness, I felt panic rise up—like I was disappearing. But then I sat with that fear, held it as I would hold a frightened child, felt embraced by the Field of Care, and suddenly the fear itself dissolved. What remained was this incredible spaciousness and freedom I had never known before."

Working With Fear and Resistance

It's natural to feel some fear or resistance when first experiencing emptiness practices. The ego-mind, sensing a threat to its familiar territory, may react with anxiety, confusion, or strong urges to distract itself.

Common Fears and How to Work With Them

"If I'm not my thoughts, who am I?" This fear of identity loss is natural but misplaced. You're not losing yourself; you're discovering a more authentic, spacious version of yourself that includes your thoughts and personality, like an insubstantial rainbow appearing and disappearing, but isn't limited by them.

"What if I become detached or uncaring?" Emptiness practice actually enhances your ability for genuine care because it releases you from defensive patterns that hinder compassion. David found he could care more effectively once he wasn't carrying everyone's problems as personal burdens.

"This feels too strange or uncomfortable." Go slowly and trust the process. Like learning any new skill, emptiness practice takes time to feel natural. Start with shorter sessions and always return to basic concentration or Field of Care practices if you feel destabilized.

"I'm afraid I'll lose my motivation or ambition." True motivation actually grows stronger when it stems from your true nature rather than ego-driven striving. You'll find yourself acting out of wisdom and love rather than fear and ambition—healing the drive that often masks spiritual homesickness.

Personal Reality and Universal Reality

One way to look at this is to remember the Two Truths—the difference between personal and universal reality. You might recall that personal reality relates to everyday life, while universal reality includes what is not limited by earthly boundaries. Both viewpoints are valid and useful in their own contexts, and achieving health and happiness involves balancing and respecting both.

In our personal reality of life and relationships, it is crucial to maintain a "healthy sense of self," self-respect, clear boundaries, and an understanding that we are worthy and lovable individuals with whom others can form meaningful connections. We all need a well-functioning ego to thrive and live well.

Loch Kelly explains, "Normal ego functions include perception, thinking, attention, memory, instincts, motor coordination, and socialization. Ego functions involve moving toward or away from things. The acts of craving ('I want') or resistance/pushing away ('I don't want') are normal feelings related to survival." When craving and avoidance become exaggerated, they lead to suffering.

However, when we are caught up only in the trappings of personal reality, we can feel scared, and the sense of spiritual homesickness becomes stronger.

We need wisdom to realize that everything changes and that, ultimately, we are all connected, even when we feel separate and divided. We must learn to accept this slowly.

From a broader perspective, we see that the concept of "body" is simply an emergent phenomenon, not as tangible and solid as it appears. While we understand why we want to be someone, why we try to protect ourselves, and why we can easily feel hurt or left out, we also realize that everything exists in relation to everything else, and we know that a field of connection underpins any sense of separation from ourselves or others.

Lost in Separate Self Mode as Spiritual Homesickness

Our spiritual homesickness often manifests as feelings of alienation and disconnection when we are stuck in "lost-in-separate-self-mode." Without a sense of interconnectedness with the "Big Everything" or the unified universe, we frequently feel lonely and scared.

While our frustration and unhappiness might be understandable, all emotions are temporary, fleeting, and ultimately insubstantial. As we begin to see this broader perspective, wisdom, kindness, and understanding naturally emerge. It is not enough to understand the broader perspective of a Field of Care conceptually. We need to feel and internalize it into our being. Then we can begin to live from that perspective. Moving from reactivity to compassion and wisdom is a gradual process that can last a lifetime or happen more quickly. *(On a Personal Note: see below)*[23]

---

[23] ***On a Personal Note**: Looking back on the passing years of my own life, I can now detect a slow growing together of the Two Truths. At first, I was most of the time in "normal life," or personal reality. At times, on retreat or on a beautiful hike, I would dip into universal reality. But those*

The Integration of Personal and Universal Reality

One of the most beautiful aspects of emptiness practice is how it allows us to live comfortably with personal reality and universal reality simultaneously.

Personal Reality:

- Your unique personality, preferences, and life circumstances
- Your relationships, responsibilities, and daily activities
- Your thoughts, emotions, and human experiences
- Your role in society and your contribution to the world

Universal Reality:

- The spacious awareness that is your essential nature
- The interconnectedness of all existence
- The groundless ground from which everything arises
- The source of wisdom, love, and creativity

---

experiences would quickly get lost when I got stressed. Even after my time in Sri Lanka and India, where I had felt fully immersed in universal reality, I lost that sense of sacredness completely when I worked as an intern in a hospital. I was so stressed then that I was close to tears almost every afternoon. Another difficult time for holding on to an experience of universal reality was when I had three little children. Even finding time to meditate was extremely difficult. I knew from my past experience and reading that universal awareness was there, but I could not feel it very often.

About 15 years ago, when I immersed myself more deeply in non-dual practices, I gradually began to maintain my awareness of universal and personal reality in tandem. Loch Kelly's glimpse practices helped, as I sprinkled them into my days. The more I got acquainted with pointing-out-style practices, the easier it became to call up the field of awareness. John Makransky helped me greatly to hold difficult feelings within Loving Awareness and to let hurts metabolize and dissolve by themselves.

Emptiness practice became one of the important pointing-out-style practices for me. They helped me return to universal reality and the feeling of Loving Awareness, especially when I had taken a hurt personally, or when I felt left out or unrecognized by others.

- The feeling of a spiritual home

Rather than choosing one or the other, emptiness practice helps us hold both simultaneously. David could still be an effective principal (personal reality) while operating from spacious awareness (universal reality). The integration of these two levels is what creates authentic spiritual maturity—healing from spiritual homesickness.

In any case, we need to extend a great deal of compassion and kindness toward ourselves and our human condition. Therefore, let's practice emptiness of self—with gentleness and warmth for ourselves.

Practice: Emptiness-of-Self with Compassion

Time needed: 8-12 minutes

Purpose: Meet your constructed self with compassion and warmth

After completing the emptiness-of-self practice above, continue with:

1. **Reflecting on the constructed self**
    - From this spacious perspective, consider how you became the solid-seeming person you've felt yourself to be
    - Notice how your mind constructed this sense of self out of necessity, fear, or the desire to please others
2. **Cultivating self-compassion**
    - Feel compassion for your younger self, doing their best to fit in, to be loved
    - Understand how this construction of yourself as a solid personality came about

3. **Reinforcing the realization**

    - Use your high-speed awareness once more to confirm there is nothing solid or independently existing about this sense of self
    - As this recedes as unfindable, affirm what remains: a field of open, spacious awareness

4. **Resting in compassionate awareness**

    - Allow yourself to be enveloped in the spaciousness of awareness
    - Stay with a sense of warmth and compassion for yourself
    - Rest in this embodied openness and spaciousness

Reflection: Feel this practice in your body, heart, and mind.

Spiritual Homesickness and the Sticky Nature of Thoughts and Emotions

The topic of "emptiness of thoughts and emotions" is complex and can lead to great feelings of spiritual homesickness. Thoughts and emotions are "sticky" and tend to cling to us. A psychiatrist friend of mine called them "tar-babies." When thoughts or emotions get stuck in our psyche, they often cause pain and discomfort.

The practice of clearing our thoughts and emotions isn't meant to make us stop thinking or turn us into emotionless robots. Quite the opposite! It simply gives us a choice in this matter instead of letting racing thoughts and strong emotions control us.

When we explore our thoughts and emotions, we may notice that, although they don't have a physical form, they do have a sense of direction. Thoughts that pass through are like beams of light, while emotions are similar to the feeling of a breeze or gust of wind. As we observe, both thoughts and emotions come and go in their own time.

I find it comforting to understand how emotions and thoughts develop because it helps me observe and feel their patterns. As a result, I am less controlled by them, which gives me a sense of freedom and lessens the feeling of spiritual homesickness.

The Physical Reality of Emotions

The difference between thoughts and emotions is that emotions are paired with physical sensations, which makes them feel very real. That's why we call them "feelings": we can literally feel them in our hearts and bodies.

For instance, I often feel anger as a tightness in my jaw or stomach, or as tension in my arms and fists. I frequently sense sadness in my chest or as a decline in energy throughout my body. Fear often makes me feel cold from head to toe, with my arms contracting. Shame makes me want to hide my face, causing my cheeks to turn red and feel warm. Pride encourages me to hold my head high, and my speech becomes more pressured and louder than usual. These examples show how emotions and bodily sensations are connected.

When we become aware of our emotions, we realize they are temporary, fleeting feelings. This lessens their power and importance over us; however, bodily sensations stick around, like the pain in our chest when we feel sad or hear upsetting news.

In Contemplative philosophy, these emotional residues are seen as the energy of manifestation or the core of being human. By understanding how our emotions develop and recognizing the energy behind them, we can cultivate kindness toward ourselves while appreciating the emotional residue of this manifestation.

For example, the emotional residue of anger can foster determination, which might be helpful. The emotional residue of sadness encourages a longing for connection, which is essential for society's functioning. The emotional residue of fear triggers alertness, especially useful in dangerous situations. The emotional residue of shame motivates us to improve ourselves. *(On a Personal Note: see below)*[24]

Even "Positive" Emotions Can Create Attachment

Positive or pleasurable emotions can be tempting. We might develop a sense of self or spiritual ego around them. Sometimes, we become attached to viewing ourselves as compassionate, generous, tidy, loving, wise, ethical, or righteous.

Conversely, emotions that seem negative, such as fear or jealousy, might be seen as undesirable, making us want to push them away. This act of grasping or pushing away, known as reactivity, is considered the root cause of all suffering in contemplative traditions. Once again, we observe the emptiness behind these fixed labels and can release them through self-compassion. As we release our grasping, we discover freedom.

Attachment to positive emotions, such as feeling "saintly" or overly righteous, can temporarily hide feelings of spiritual homesickness. However, as they create a "false high," spiritual homesickness often returns more intensely when the bubble of self-inflation bursts.

---

[24] ***On a Personal Note:*** *I have been reflecting on these emotional residues for myself. I frequently experience social and political anger. Instead of turning inward and feeling hopeless, or hurting someone who I feel is responsible, I have learned to turn my frustration into action and engagement. I go to protests and write essays for the local newspaper. My great sadness over the suffering in this country and the world is transformed by me starting new meditation groups, or giving retreats, as I feel this helps others not to lose heart. We need safe places and community.*

I have also been thinking of self-improvement and creativity as a response to shame. As the little girl in post-war Germany without a father, a child of refugees, I felt plenty of shame. The worst was when mothers of friends asked about my non-existent father. My long psychological and spiritual journey may have had, at least partly, the aspect of digging myself out of the hole of shame through growing, learning, and transforming myself, by becoming a "wounded healer."

My student Maria once told me, “I thought I was supposed to be this perfectly compassionate person who never gets angry. I was so attached to being ‘spiritual’ that I couldn’t be human anymore! Emptiness practice helped me see that my ‘spiritual self’ was just another construct, and I could let that go too. Now I can be angry sometimes without it defining me, and I can be loving without needing to be perfect.”

Practice: Emptiness-of-Thoughts and Emotions

Time needed: 7 minutes

Purpose: Discover the insubstantial nature of thoughts and emotions while honoring their energy.

Begin with the emptiness-of-self practice above, then:

1. **Examine your thoughts**

    - Notice your thoughts and familiar thinking patterns
    - Use high-speed awareness to search for anything solid or substantial in them
    - As thoughts show themselves as fleeting, affirm what persists: open, spacious awareness.

2. **Work with emotions**

    - Bring an emotion into your awareness (a familiar emotion that often grips you)
    - It might be painful (anxiety, anger, fear, or shame) or positive (attached love)
    - Recall how this emotion feels in your body
    - Allow yourself to sense the bodily feelings that accompany this emotion

3. **Search for solidity in emotions**

    - Make a high-speed search through this emotion and its bodily sensations
    - Look for anything solid, permanent, or independently existing
    - Notice how nothing solid can be found
    - See how it dissipates like a breeze or gust of wind

4. **Rest in awareness with care**

    - Affirm what remains: spaciousness, the field quality of awareness itself
    - While held in awareness, stay with a sense of warmth and care for yourself

5. **Recognize the energy of emotions**

    - Gently feel the emotion once more, including its visceral quality
    - Notice the energetic residue, its energy of manifestation

6. **Recognize the positive aspect of emotions**

    - Recognize that
        - The residue of sadness is a longing for connection
        - The residue of anger is determination
        - The residue of fear is attentiveness
        - The residue of shame is trying to be your best self
    - If even that positive residue still has a charge, release it
    - Affirm what remains: the energy of awareness
    - Rest in it, as a quality of depth, of the ground of being, of your spiritual home

Reflection: Feel this practice in your body, heart, and mind.

Key Insight: Emotions are not eliminated but expressed as energy manifestations of awareness. Their wisdom remains, even as their sticky, solid form dissolves.

Modulating Intensity: If emotions become overwhelming, return to the Field of Care practice. Allow difficult feelings to be held in Loving Awareness before exploring their nature.

Glimpse Practices for Everyday Use

Emptiness-of-Thought Glimpse

(adapted from Loch Kelly)

Time needed: 1-2 minutes

Purpose: Quickly recognizing when thoughts are insubstantial during the day while caught in mental loops

Practice:

- Feel your body as a whole, the felt sense of your whole entire body
- Imagine your whole body to be lit up with awareness, very inch, every particle of your body alive and awake
- Then feel the focuser, the thinking mind, in your forehead
- Be the focuser, the thinking mind
- Move from forehead to jaw and feel the jaw from the inside out
- Unhook from the jaw
- Let awareness drop into your heart
- Feel the felt sense of awareness as heart from the inside out
- Move awareness to the back of your heart, and feel the felt sense in the back of your heart

- Feel awareness in the back of your body, and slowly let awareness wrap around your whole body
- Rest in awareness
- Now, while resting in awareness, notice thoughts passing through like rays of light, insubstantial yet occurring
- Notice their passing nature and affirm what remains—only spacious emptiness

Reflection: Feel this practice in your body, heart, and mind.

Emptiness-of-Feeling Glimpse

Time needed: 1-2 minutes

Purpose: During your days, quickly recognize when emotions are insubstantial, after you had been caught in feeling loops

Practice:

- Feel your body as a whole, the felt sense of your whole entire body
- Imagine your whole body to be lit up with awareness, very inch, every particle of your body alive and awake
- Then feel the focuser, the thinking mind, in your forehead
- Be the focuser, the thinking mind
- Move from forehead to jaw and feel the jaw from the inside out
- Unhook from the jaw
- Let awareness drop into your heart
- Feel the felt sense of awareness as heart from the inside out
- Move awareness to the back of your heart, and feel the felt sense in the back of your heart
- Feel awareness in the back of your body, and slowly let awareness wrap around your whole body

- Rest in awareness
- Now, while resting in awareness, pull up a strong emotion
- Feel how that emotion manifests as body feeling
- From the place of awareness, investigate if the emotion is substantial
- Roam around and see if there is anything solid or permanent
- Affirm what remains, only spacious awareness

Reflection: Feel this practice in your body, heart, and mind.

Use this practice when stuck in repetitive thought or strong feelings, before important conversations, or whenever mental activity feels intense and overwhelming

Emptiness in Daily Life: Practical Applications

1. Dealing with Criticism or Praise

When someone criticizes you, instead of immediately identifying as "the one being criticized," pause and ask: "Who is the one hearing this criticism?" Often, you'll discover that the spacious awareness receiving the feedback is much less reactive than the constructed self.

2. Making Decisions

Rather than struggling with decisions from the perspective of "What should I do?" try shifting to "What wants to emerge here?" This opens space for wisdom to arise naturally rather than forcing solutions through mental effort.

3. Handling Stress

When feeling overwhelmed, practice the gentle inquiry: "Who is the one feeling stressed?" This can create immediate space around the stressful experience, allowing for more skillful responses.

4. Relationships

In conflicts, ask: "Who is the one feeling hurt or angry?" This practice can shift you from reactive patterns to responsive presence, often transforming the entire dynamic of the interaction.

5. Work and Service

As David discovered, emptiness practice can boost your effectiveness at work by freeing you from the ego's need to control outcomes. You can act from wisdom and care instead of self-importance or fear—offering a more authentic healing presence to our spiritually homesick world.

Deepening the Practice: Advanced Inquiries

As you become more comfortable with basic emptiness inquiry, you can delve into subtler aspects.

The Emptiness of Thoughts: "What is a thought made of? Where do thoughts come from, and where do they go? Who thinks the thoughts?"

The Emptiness of Emotions: "What is an emotion when I'm not telling myself a story about it? Where does anger actually exist when I look for it directly?"

The Emptiness of Time: "Where is the past right now? Where is the future? What is this moment when I'm not thinking about it?"

The Emptiness of the Body: " What is the felt sense of the body when I'm not imaging it visually?"

Each of these questions can enhance your understanding of the built nature of experience and help you become more aware of the open awareness that is always there.

Signs of Progress in Emptiness Practice

As your practice develops, you may observe:

- Greater flexibility in how you see yourself and situations
- Reduced reactivity to criticism or praise
- Natural development of compassion for others' suffering
- Ability to stay calm in chaotic situations
- Spontaneous insights that come effortlessly
- Sense of "effortless effectiveness" in everyday activities
- Increasing freedom from trying to control results
- Great relief from the pressure of upholding a strict self-image
- Healing the deep loneliness that defines spiritual homesickness.

The Paradox of Selflessness

One of the most beautiful paradoxes of practicing emptiness is that as you let go of your grip on the separate self, you don't lose your individuality—you discover your true nature. Free from the confines of rigid self-concepts, your unique gifts and qualities can express themselves more fully and naturally. You are closer to home.

David didn't become less of a leader through emptiness practice; he became a more genuine and effective leader. His care for his students didn't lessen; it deepened because it was no longer filtered through his ego's need to maintain a certain image.

This is the promise of emptiness practice: not the loss of self, but the discovery of your true Self—the spacious, wise, compassionate awareness that is your deepest identity and your true home beyond spiritual homesickness. From this foundation, you can engage with life more fully, love more freely, and serve others with effortless effectiveness that arises when action flows from your essential nature rather than from your constructed personality.

In the next chapter, we'll examine how recognizing our true nature can become a living reality through practices that help us "taste the field" of Loving Awareness directly, making it a constant source of wisdom and nourishment for our daily lives and our service to a world longing for spiritual connection.

CHAPTER 6

Tasting the Ground of Being

Once we have glimpsed the fluid, spacious nature of our separate self through emptiness practice, a natural question arises: How do we turn this recognition of Loving Awareness into a lived experience rather than just an occasional peak? This chapter explores practices that help us "taste the field" of awareness directly, making it accessible in every moment of our lives—providing ongoing healing for spiritual homesickness.

This practice provides healing for spiritual homesickness by offering direct access to our true home—the ground of being that is always closer than we think. By learning to experience the field of Loving Awareness firsthand, we realize that what we've been searching for has never really been absent, healing the core disconnection that defines spiritual displacement.

Elena's Story: From Seeking to Being

Elena, a 38-year-old environmental scientist, had spent years attending meditation retreats, reading spiritual books, and practicing different forms of contemplation. Despite her efforts, she often felt like awareness was something she had to work hard to reach—a distant mountain peak she occasionally glimpsed but could never quite attain.

"I have all these wonderful experiences during retreats," she explained during one of our sessions, "but then I go back to my normal life and it feels like I've lost the connection. I find myself chasing those peak states again, which creates this exhausting cycle of spiritual striving."

Elena's frustration revealed a common challenge in spiritual practice—seeing awareness as something to achieve rather than recognizing it as the foundation of everyday experience. Like many dedicated practitioners, she was experiencing a form of spiritual homesickness: craving transcendent states while feeling disconnected from the sacred in daily life.

Her work as a climate researcher added to this challenge. "I spend my days analyzing data about ecosystem collapse and rising temperatures," she said. "It's meaningful work, but it's also overwhelming. I know meditation is supposed to help, but most of the time I feel like I need to escape from reality rather than engage with it more deeply."

Elena was struggling with what many spiritual seekers face: the gap between formal practice and daily life, between peak experiences and ordinary consciousness. She sought relief from the burden of environmental grief rather than learning to embrace that grief with an open heart.

I introduced Elena to what I call "field of awareness" practices—simple ways of recognizing that Loving Awareness isn't something we need to create or achieve, but something we can taste directly in each moment, even while engaged in challenging work. These practices are meant to heal the divide between spiritual practice and daily engagement.

"Let's start with something very simple," I suggested. "Right now, as you're sitting here, notice that you're aware. You're aware of my voice, aware of your thoughts about what I'm saying, aware of the feeling of the chair supporting you. Can you feel into the awareness that's noticing all of this?"

Elena paused, her brow furrowing with concentration. "I think so... but it feels like I'm trying to grasp something that's not really there."

"That's the key insight," I replied. "Awareness isn't something to grab onto—it's what's doing the noticing right now. Instead of reaching for it, can you simply be it? You don't have to achieve awareness; you are awareness, aware of all these experiences. It's like making a backward step."

I guided Elena through a simple practice: "Instead of searching for awareness as an object, notice that you are the space where all experiences happen. Your thoughts, emotions, and sensations—they all come up within the space of awareness that you are."

Something shifted in Elena's expression. "Oh," she said softly. "It's not somewhere else. It's... here. It's what I am, not what I have."

This was Elena's first direct experience of what contemplatives call "rigpa" or "primary awareness"—the understanding that awareness isn't a separate state we enter but our core nature. Over the next few weeks, I showed her simple practices for recognizing this awareness in her daily life.

"When you're analyzing climate data," I suggested, "instead of getting lost in the content of what you're studying, occasionally notice the awareness that takes in all this information. Who or what is it that knows these temperature readings? What is the space in which concern about climate change arises?"

Elena started trying out these micro-practices during her workday. Instead of viewing her environmental concerns as barriers to spiritual peace, she began seeing them as acts of care emerging from awareness itself.

"Something remarkable happened yesterday," she reported during our next session. "I was reading a particularly devastating report about coral reef die-offs, and instead of getting overwhelmed or trying to detach from the feelings, I asked myself: 'What is aware of this grief?'

"Suddenly, there was a vast space around the sadness—not pushing it away, but holding it within something much larger. The grief was still there, but it was contained within this incredible tenderness. I could feel my heart breaking open with love for these ecosystems rather than closing down with despair."

This was a crucial breakthrough for Elena. She was learning to see the field of awareness not as a way to escape difficult emotions but as a loving space that could hold all experiences with compassion—healing her spiritual homesickness by recognizing the sacred within her everyday concerns.

Over the following months, Elena's relationship with both her spiritual practice and her work changed in surprising ways. Instead of needing to escape to retreats to find peace, she realized that Loving Awareness was just as present while reviewing scientific papers, attending climate conferences, or having difficult conversations with colleagues about environmental policy.

"The strangest thing," she reflected, "is that I'm actually more effective at my work now, not less. When I operate from this state of awareness, I can process difficult information without becoming overwhelmed. I can handle challenging conversations without reacting. It's as if I have access to a deeper intelligence that knows how to respond wisely to each situation."

Elena realized what many practitioners eventually understand: Loving Awareness isn't a special state we attain through spiritual practices, but the very foundation of everyday experience. When we learn to directly experience this field, our daily lives become expressions of awakened presence rather than barriers to it—offering deep healing for spiritual homesickness.

As we heal our own spiritual homesickness through these practices, we naturally become medicine for others suffering from the same collective disconnection. Elena's transformation allowed her to serve the environmental movement from a place of sustainable love rather than urgent desperation.

The Field of Loving Awareness

Elena's journey reveals an important truth: Loving Awareness isn't distant or hard to access—it's so close to our experience that we often overlook it. Like eyes that see everything except themselves, awareness is the foundation through which all experiences happen, yet we rarely recognize it directly.

Think about this moment now: You are aware of these words, aware of your surroundings, and aware of your thoughts about what you're reading. This awareness isn't located somewhere specific—it's the open space where all these experiences happen. You don't have to travel anywhere to find awareness; you just need to recognize what is already deeply present.

Awareness Is Closer Than We Think

Let's explore ways to more fully open ourselves to what I call the "field quality" of Loving Awareness. I've already mentioned several gateways: through deep concentration in focusing practice, through emptiness-of-self practices, through glimpse practices, through devotional openings, or by recognizing those spontaneous moments of awareness that sometimes arise unexpectedly in our daily lives. Contemplatives described a step-by-step process for entering the timeless quality of awareness.

Remember, Loving Awareness isn't a "thing" we create or acquire. As my colleague Loch Kelly reminds his students, it's more like "a quantum field made of nothing, which has the qualities of particles and waves. It contains no content, yet events arise in it. It holds the nuances of love and knowing." At its core, it is beyond substance yet undeniably present.

This Loving Awareness is always present. It has always existed and will always be there whenever we rise above the clouds of our personal selves, with all their thoughts and worries. Our experience varies depending on how deeply we connect with it. The awareness itself remains constant, but our understanding of it can expand.

One potential pitfall I've noticed is that focusing too much on ourselves, whether through mindfulness or psychotherapy, can sometimes turn self-focus into an end in itself. This might actually strengthen our identification with ourselves and deepen our sense of separation from others. Loch Kelly says that the experience of getting stuck in one's psychological process, and one's rumination about self-identity, can lead to what he calls a "psychological underpass." When we learn to unhook our awareness from our thinking mind centered in the forehead, we can experience awareness as something much larger. This allows us to enter the realm of Loving Awareness, which naturally expands on its own.

When awareness starts to rest in itself, we experience the interconnected web of life. From this perspective, as Loch Kelly describes it, "The field of awareness, the phenomena arising in it, and the moment of perceiving this are flowing together and mutually co-arising." Through open-hearted awareness, we simultaneously feel connected and protected, vulnerable yet courageous, and motivated to create and relate. Wisdom and love become fully present, along with a natural desire to help all beings who are suffering.

The Awareness That's Been Here All Along

While Loving Awareness goes beyond personal identity—it's a "no-thing" that's fundamentally present—we often experience it personally as it flows through our lives. Have you ever noticed how little babies seem to stay connected with this field of awareness? The unconscious process of building a personal identity begins only around 18 months old. When babies are born, they might feel like they've left home. As we grow through childhood into our teens and adulthood, emotions and external stimuli often take over our awareness. Still, that subtle homesickness we sometimes feel is usually a longing to return to this natural state.

Our goal isn't to create something new but to remember (or "re-member") Loving Awareness as our fundamental operating system. As we do this, our personal sense of self fades into the background. It stays accessible when needed, but no longer governs us. Living within this new system, we gradually realize that the stillness of Loving Awareness and the lively phenomena of life are simply two aspects of the same reality, like an ocean and its waves. It is not enough to understand the broader perspective of a Field of Care conceptually. We need to feel and internalize it into our being. Then we can begin to live from that perspective. Together, there is a wholeness that has always existed, even when hidden and unrecognized.

Experiencing this Loving Awareness is relatively easy, but maintaining it in our lives requires remembering and focus. One approach is to practice brief glimpses throughout the day, cultivating a habit that, through neuroplasticity, gradually opens a neural pathway to support this awareness. Stabilization takes time, but with diligent practice, motivation, and trust, it develops. Over time, we become like homing pigeons, effortlessly finding our way back to what has always been our true nature.

Characteristics of the Field of Awareness

1. **Always Present:** Awareness never comes and goes. It's the constant background of all experience, like the sky that's always there, whether cloudy or clear.

2. **Spacious:** Unlike thoughts or emotions that have boundaries, awareness is inherently open and unlimited, capable of containing any experience without being disturbed by it.
3. **Knowing:** Awareness isn't blank or unconscious—it's a luminous knowing presence that recognizes whatever arises within it.
4. **Peaceful:** In its natural state, awareness is inherently at ease, undisturbed by the changing content of experience.
5. **Loving:** When we taste awareness directly, we often discover it has a quality of unconditional love and acceptance for whatever appears within it—the ultimate medicine for spiritual homesickness.
6. **Timeless:** Loving Awareness is not constrained by time, it is always now.
7. **Formless:** The ground of Loving Awareness is insubstantial, it has no form. Phenomena are arising in it and are dissolving again.
8. **Non-local:** The ground of Loving Awareness has no place, it is everywhere and always. It is always "here, now." *(On a Personal Note: see below)*[25]

---

[25] ***On a Personal Note:*** *Through my years to studying vipassana—insight or ordinary mindfulness meditation, (it goes by many names)—I had various experiences of the Field of Awareness, but I did not know I had them. I felt stillness, bliss, timelessness, and boundlessness, even love, but could not name what it was. Often I disregarded such experiences because they did not fit into my scientifically schooled mind.*

You might ask, why does it help to learn about it? First, so we do not disregard a precious experience or feel weird about having it. Then it helped me to get to know the (ultimate) reality of it. I learned to know that this Loving Awareness is something I can trust, I can long for, and I can experience through my felt sense. Psychologist William James said: What we pay attention to becomes reality. Through paying attention to it, Lowing Awareness and I formed a relationship, even though I related neither to a person nor a thing. I allowed this "Great Mystery" to become important to me, to love it and be loved by it. This, in turn, allowed me to feel safe with it. I knew, if I remember it, that the Great Mystery remembers me. I can feel this love in my body and my heart. Having been wounded by the Catholic Church (they did not like unwed mothers and their children), I

Simple Practices to Taste the Field

The following practices are designed to help you recognize the field of awareness directly, making it accessible throughout your daily life.

Practice: Awareness Aware of Itself

Time needed: 2-5 minutes

Purpose: Direct recognition of awareness as your fundamental nature—this practice offers healing for spiritual homesickness by revealing that you are the home you've been seeking

Instructions:

1. Sit comfortably and notice that you are aware right now
2. Instead of focusing on what you're aware of (thoughts, sensations, sounds), turn attention to the awareness itself
3. Ask yourself: "What is it that's aware of my thoughts?"
4. Notice that awareness can't be located or grasped—it's the space in which everything appears
5. Simply be this awareness, aware of being aware
6. If thoughts arise, recognize them as movements within awareness, like clouds in the sky
7. Rest as the sky-like awareness that remains unchanged by whatever passes through it

Reflection: Feel this practice in your body, heart, and mind.

Key insight: You don't need to attain awareness—you just need to realize that you are awareness, right now.

---

was grateful to connect to the sacred in a secular way. I did not need to belong to a church or temple to experience the sacred. It is now, limitless and boundless, always here.

Practice: From Deliberate to Effortless Awareness

(Glimpse adapted from Loch Kelly)

Time needed: 1-3 minutes

Purpose: This practice invites recognition of itself directly. We shift from mindfulness to Loving Awareness itself. Recognize awareness as the witness of all experience—healing spiritual homesickness by discovering the ground of being, the stable presence that is always home.

Instructions:

1. Feel your seat on the chair or cushion, feet on the ground.
2. Notice your breath moving in and out on its own. Feel the sensation of breathing.
3. Include sounds in the room, the play of light through your eyes, any tastes or smells.
4. Now ask gently: What is it that is aware of all these sensations, thoughts, and feelings?
5. Let the question open rather than searching for an answer.
6. Allow awareness to turn back, as if turning back at its own face. Notice that awareness itself is present—open, clear, already here.
7. Rest not as the observer of awareness, but as awareness itself—effortless, boundless, naturally aware.

Reflection: Feel this practice in your body, heart, and mind.

Daily life application: Use this practice while walking, driving, or any time your eyes are open. Let ordinary seeing become a gateway to recognizing awareness.

Deepening Practices to Taste the Field of Awareness

"Letting Be," a simple Dzogchen Style of Tasting the Groundless Ground

The Groundless Ground, or however we want to call the great mystery, is the source of the qualities of goodness, such as love or care, knowing or wisdom, spaciousness, and luminosity or boundlessness. By allowing us to be drawn into this depth, we get access to and ultimately unify with the qualities of this field of Awake Loving Awareness.

With the Letting Be meditation, adapted from John Makransky, we learn to relax into it and allow ourselves to be drawn into this profound depth. In some ways, this meditation also serves as an emptiness-of-self practice. To be drawn into this depth, we must relinquish our sense-of-self and our control; we need to fully let go for this practice. When we learn to do that, we nurture our longing that this depth will be the secure ground from which to live our lives.

Practice: Letting Be

Time needed: 10-15 minutes

Purpose: Surrender into the groundless ground of being

1. **Settle into body and breath**

   - Come down from thinking mind into your body
   - Leave your eyes slightly open, yet fully relaxed
   - Let your belly breathe
   - While relaxing and completely letting go with each exhale

2. **Letting be of body**

- Allow awareness to fill your whole body and your whole body be drawn into the depth of awareness
- Sensations of body, including tightness or discomfort, are felt as awareness
- Body as a whole field of awareness is relaxing, letting be
- Let the body do the meditating
- Body and awareness are one unified field of experience
- Be drawn into depth

3. Letting be of breath

- Each outbreath is drawing you into deep relaxation, letting be
- Breath is experienced as awareness, and awareness as breath
- Let depth draw breath more and more into itself
- Fully surrender to depth, just letting be, until the next breath brushes in naturally
- Let breath do the meditating
- Awareness, breath, and body are one unified field of experience in depth

4. Letting be of mind

- Open your eyes, and look ahead with a panoramic gaze, filling the whole visual field
- Leave all senses wide open, relaxing into this panoramic visual field
- When there is grasping or contracting of the mind, let that feeling relax deeply and be drawn into depth
- When thoughts arise, let depth draw awareness into the spaces between thoughts
- Let depth do the meditating
- Rest in this awareness between thoughts, these spaces of openness

5. Settle into the background of mind

- Settle back, inwardly resting in the background of awareness, which is naturally open and luminous like a bright summer sky
- Let mind, awareness, and space become one unified field of experience in depth
- If thoughts or sounds arise, let them dissolve, being drawn into depth
- Let awareness do the meditating
- Let everything be

Reflection: Feel this practice in your body, heart, and mind.

Pointing-Out-Style Practice: A Mahamudra Approach to Tasting Awake Loving Awareness

For further exploration of Loving Awareness, the following Pointing-Out-Style practice from the Tibetan Mahamudra tradition can be particularly powerful. This practice is most effective when you have 15 to 20 minutes for a more formal meditation session.

Begin by aligning your posture, with your eyes slightly open and gazing downward, and deepen your mind through focused breathing. Set an intention for your practice, perhaps dedicating any benefits to the well-being of all beings. Feel your longing for home in your heart. It may pull you along like a magnet. Trust in yourself, your ability to practice, and in life itself. Connect with your heart, allowing your awareness to stay there, here and now. You've reached the "Mount Everest Basecamp" and are ready to start the climb.

Practice: Mahamudra Style for Tasting Awake Awareness

Time needed: 10 minutes

Purpose: experiencing the particular, here the breath, on the ground of Loving Awareness

1. **Settle into body and breath** using the 3-point-breath (inbreath, outbreath, and body as a whole)

2. **Develop concentration**

   - Concentrate, intensify, and ease up until you can stay solidly with your breath
   - Maintain a continuous flow, allowing breath to move automatically
   - If distracted, stabilize even more
   - Intensify and ease your breath into an awake, relaxed flow
   - Notice how focusing continues automatically
   - Stay evenly and steadily with the breath,
   - Let yourself be breathed
   - You are now resting in the subtler level of mind

3. **Open to the field of awareness**

   - Open your eyes slightly, keeping them relaxed and unfocused
   - Hold the view of light flooding through you, connecting inside with outside
   - Shift awareness to the space around you
   - Mix the space of awareness with awareness, and awareness with space, so everything is filled with awareness, made of awareness, open, wide-awakeness, filled with warmth
   - Linger in this feeling of resting in awareness, as awareness, open, wide-awakeness

4. **Recognize the non-dual nature of awareness**

   - Take the view that you're surrounded by this wide-awake field of Loving Awareness

- This luminous field saturates everything—no inside, no outside
- Feel how everything in this field is open, empty, filled with warmth
- Sounds are open and empty; thoughts and feelings are open and empty
- Awareness, objects, and your perception of those objects are open and insubstantial
- The field of awareness is like the vast, boundless sky

5. **Rest in awareness while remaining with the breath**

- From this open perspective, follow the movement and sensation of the rising breath and the falling breath
- Between the outbreath and inbreath, rest in the vast field of open, awake awareness, suffused with warmth
- Follow this gentle rhythm—inbreath, outbreath, vast field of awareness
- Rest in this simple, always-present reality

6. **Surrender to the natural flow**

- Follow the rising breath closely, moment by moment, and the falling breath, relaxed yet keenly attentive
- Surrender to breath arising by itself out of the field of awareness, and falling back into it
- Allow this process to flow by itself as energy and light, breath as energy, energy as breath
- Rest in spaciousness and vastness, held in Loving Awareness

Reflection: Feel this practice in your body, heart, and mind.

This practice helps integrate the focused attention developed through concentration with the open, spacious quality of Loving Awareness. You will stabilize your taste of home. Through this integration, you learn how to simultaneously hold both precise attention and boundless awareness—like an eagle that maintains both a keen focus on specific details and a vast perspective of the entire landscape.

Practice: Awareness During Activities

Time needed: Throughout daily activities

Purpose: Integrate recognition of awareness into ordinary tasks—healing existential distress and spiritual doubts by making every moment a path back to home

Instructions:

While eating:

- Be aware of the awareness that tastes the food
- Feel the flavors and textures
- Eat from the space of awareness itself

While listening:

- Be aware of the awareness that hears sounds
- Feel pleasant or unpleasant sounds
- Rest as the space in which all sounds arise and dissolve

While walking:

- Feel the awareness that knows the body's movement
- Walk from awareness rather than from the sense of being a separate walker

While thinking:

- Be aware of the awareness that observes thoughts
- Be the awareness in which thoughts appear
- Rest as the space of awareness that remains peaceful regardless of thought content

Reflection: Feel this practice in your body, heart, and mind.

Key insight: Any ordinary activity can become a doorway to recognizing Loving Awareness when we shift from identifying with the doer to resting as the aware presence within which all doing occurs

Working with Resistance and Obstacles

As you begin practicing these "taste the field" exercises, you may encounter some common challenges.

"I can't find awareness—it's too subtle": This is actually a good sign! Awareness is so intimate and immediate that our usual way of looking for objects can't locate it. Try shifting from searching for awareness as a "thing" to simply being the awareness that's looking.

"My mind is too busy to rest in awareness": Awareness isn't affected by a busy mind any more than the sky is affected by weather. Notice that even chaotic thoughts arise within the spacious awareness that you are. You don't need a quiet mind to recognize awareness. In fact, concentration becomes much easier from the perspective of awareness.

"This feels boring or nothing special": Our minds are conditioned to seek dramatic experiences, but awareness is often subtle and ordinary. The "nothing special" quality is actually a sign that you're recognizing Loving Awareness as your natural state rather than as a peak experience to achieve.

"I keep forgetting to notice Loving Awareness": This is normal. Set gentle reminders throughout your day—when your phone buzzes, when you open doors, when you take your first sip of coffee. Each moment of remembering to notice awareness is valuable, regardless of how often you forget.

"I worry I'm just spacing out or dissociating": Resting in Loving Awareness is very different from spacing out. In awareness, there's a clear, alert presence that's fully available to whatever is happening. If you feel foggy or disconnected, go back to basic concentration exercises or grounding in physical sensations.

The Integration of Awakened and Ordinary Awareness

One of the most beautiful discoveries in "tasting the field" is realizing that there's no fundamental difference between Loving Awareness and ordinary consciousness. Elena discovered this when she stopped trying to escape her environmental work and instead found Loving Awareness present within her scientific analysis and climate grief.

Ordinary Awareness:

- Paying attention to daily tasks and responsibilities
- Responding to work emails, managing household duties
- Engaging in conversations and problem-solving
- Feeling emotions and having thoughts about daily life

Loving Awareness:

- The same daily activities, but recognized as expressions of awareness
- Working from spacious presence rather than contracted effort
- Emotions and thoughts held within Loving Awareness
- Natural wisdom arises to guide responses and decisions

The goal isn't to replace ordinary awareness with some special "awakened" state, but to recognize that ordinary experience is already occurring within the field of Loving Awareness. This integration heals the split between spiritual practice and daily life that creates much of our spiritual homesickness.

Awareness in Challenging Situations

Some of the most profound opportunities to taste the field of awareness come during difficult moments. Elena's breakthrough came while reading about ecological destruction—not despite the challenging content, but because of how she related to it from awareness.

During Emotional Difficulty: Instead of being overwhelmed by strong emotions, feel them from Loving Awareness. Notice that awareness itself remains spacious and peaceful even when containing powerful emotional energy. Loving Awareness may even increase in intensity.

During Physical Pain: Rather than fighting discomfort, rest in awareness, while expanding into spaciousness. Often, you'll discover that Loving Awareness can hold pain with compassion without being diminished by it.

During Mental Agitation: When the mind is racing with worry or confusion, rest as the still, spacious, Loving Awareness within which mental agitation appears and dissolves.

During Conflict: In interpersonal tension, step back and rest in Loving Awareness. From the space of awareness, you can respond to challenging behavior without taking it personally or becoming reactive.

During Spiritual Homesickness: When that deep longing for meaning arises, pause and rest in Loving Awareness. Often, you'll find that the awareness longing for home is itself the home you've been searching for.

The Ripple Effects of Tasting Awareness

As you become more familiar with recognizing and resting in the field of Loving Awareness, you might notice several natural developments:

Enhanced Presence: Others may comment that you seem more "there" when they're with you. This presence isn't something you're doing; it's Loving Awareness naturally expressing itself through your engagement.

Effortless Effectiveness: As Elena found in her environmental work, operating from Loving Awareness often enhances your skills and creativity rather than diminishing your engagement. Solutions come naturally; suitable responses appear without forced thinking.

Emotional Resilience: Difficult emotions can still arise, but they're held within the larger space of Loving Awareness rather than defining your entire experience. For example, you can feel grief about climate change without being overwhelmed by despair.

Spontaneous Compassion: As Loving Awareness recognizes itself in all beings, care for others arises naturally. This isn't forced kindness but the organic expression of recognizing your essential interconnectedness—natural medicine for our collectively spiritually homesick world.

Wisdom in Action: Decisions originate from intuitive wisdom instead of mental struggle. You naturally know what's needed in each situation without having to figure it out logically.

Freedom from Spiritual Seeking: The exhausting search for enlightenment or peak experiences gradually fades as you realize that what you're seeking is already present as your own aware nature—complete healing of spiritual homesickness.

Living as the Field

The ultimate "taste" of Loving Awareness occurs when recognition becomes so natural that you no longer see yourself as someone who occasionally accesses awareness, but as Loving Awareness itself, temporarily expressing through a specific body-mind. This isn't a dramatic shift but a subtle settling into what has always been true.

Elena expressed this beautifully: "I used to think of myself as Elena, who sometimes experienced moments of Loving Awareness. Now it's more like Loving Awareness is expressing itself as Elena's life—studying climate data, caring about coral reefs, having conversations with colleagues. It's all Loving Awareness in different forms."

This recognition doesn't make you less human or take away your personality—quite the opposite. Free from the limits of a rigid separate self, your true nature can express itself more openly and naturally. Your unique talents, interests, and ways of caring for the world become expressions of Loving Awareness rather than burdens of a separate self. *(On a Personal Note: see below)*[26]

Integration Practices for Daily Life

To help make "tasting the field" a continuous reality rather than an occasional practice, consider these ongoing approaches:

---

[26] ***On a Personal Note:*** *During her last year of life, when she was 95, I had a wonderful discussion with my dear friend and mentor Joanna Macy. I asked her if we were all becoming the same, a bland group of folks, as we are reaching high levels of awareness. I was worried that we would lose our uniqueness, our interesting particularity. I was worried that, in our interdependence, we would all become the same, without distinction.*

Joanna gave a wonderful answer to my concern. She spoke about "mutual differentiation," meaning that the more we realize our interconnectedness and our reality as an aspect of the Field of Awareness, the more we can be ourselves, each in our unique, colorful expressions. However, this uniqueness was now not emerging from ego, but from the spontaneous expression of our love and creativity.

Morning Intention: Before getting out of bed, spend a moment recognizing the awareness that is aware of waking up. Set an intention to notice this Loving Awareness throughout the day.

Transition Moments: Use doorways, traffic lights, or phone notifications as reminders to pause and savor the warmth of awareness in which these experiences occur.

Work Integration: Whether you're a scientist like Elena, a teacher, a parent, or engaged in any activity, occasionally remind yourself to step back and to rest in Loving Awareness itself.

Evening Reflection: Before sleep, recall moments during the day when you remembered to rest in Loving Awareness. Appreciate these moments without judging times when you forgot. When you fall asleep, step back and rest in Loving Awareness.

Relationship Practice: During conversations, occasionally notice the warmth and wisdom of awareness that's listening and speaking. Can you engage with others from this space of aware presence?

In the next chapter, we'll explore how recognizing ourselves as the field of Loving Awareness changes our understanding of the connection between the personal and universal parts of our experience—learning to be both the wave and the ocean at the same time. This provides deep healing for spiritual homesickness by revealing our true home in the vast field of Loving Awareness.

CHAPTER 7

Ocean and Waves—The Unity of Individual and Universal

Now that we've learned to taste the field of awareness directly, a beautiful paradox emerges: How can we be both the vast ocean of Loving Awareness and the individual wave of our personal experience simultaneously? This chapter explores one of the most profound recognitions in contemplative spirituality—the non-dual understanding that wave and ocean are not separate, but different expressions of the same essential nature. This recognition offers a surprising healing for spiritual homesickness by revealing that we have never actually been separate from our true home.

This practice offers healing for spiritual homesickness by revealing the final piece of the triple medicine: we can live as both individual expressions and universal awareness simultaneously, eliminating the challenging choice between personal life and spiritual awakening that often leads to a sense of spiritual alienation.

Marcus's Story: The Executive Who United with the Wateriness of Life

Marcus, a 52-year-old CEO of a mid-sized technology company, attended my teachings carrying what he described as "two different lives that don't seem to connect." On one side, he was deeply committed to his morning meditation practice and had experienced profound states of unity during silent retreats. On the other side, his business world was completely separate from these spiritual experiences—a realm of quarterly reports, board meetings, and tough decisions that seemed to require what he called his "armor of professionalism."

"It's like I'm two different people," Marcus explained during our first session. "There's the Marcus who feels these incredible moments of peace and unity during meditation, and then there's the CEO Marcus who has to make tough decisions, sometimes letting people go and navigating corporate politics. I can't figure out how to bring these two worlds together."

Marcus was feeling a typical kind of spiritual homesickness—the painful divide between transcendent experiences and worldly responsibilities, between the calm of meditation and the complexities of human relationships and work demands.

His dilemma had grown more intense recently as his company faced the need for significant layoffs because of market changes. "How can I be talking about universal love and interconnectedness one moment, and then the next be deciding which employees to let go? It feels hypocritical, like I'm living a lie."

This split was causing immense stress for Marcus. His meditation practice, instead of supporting his daily life, had become an escape from it. He found himself craving retreat environments where he could connect with what felt like his "true self," while viewing his business responsibilities as somehow "less spiritual" or even obstacles to his awakening.

I introduced Marcus to the ocean and wave teaching—the idea that we don't have to choose between being the vast oceanic awareness and being the individual wave of our personal experience. Just like water that expresses itself as both ocean and wave at the same time, we can be both the limitless field of Loving Awareness and the unique expression of that awareness living as Marcus's specific life.

"Think of it this way," I suggested. "The wave never stops being ocean, even while it has its own distinct shape and movement. The ocean expresses itself through countless individual waves, each unique, but none separate from the ocean itself. You don't have to transcend being Marcus to rest in universal awareness—Marcus is how universal awareness is expressing itself right now."

We started exploring practices that helped Marcus recognize both aspects of his experience simultaneously. Instead of trying to escape his role as CEO to reach awareness, he learned to notice awareness manifesting through his leadership duties.

"During your next board meeting," I suggested, "instead of trying to be someone other than who you are, feel the awareness that is aware of this meeting. Can you speak and listen from that awareness rather than from anxiety about outcomes?"

Marcus was initially skeptical. "But these are serious business decisions that affect people's livelihoods. I can't just zone out and hope everything works out."

"I'm not suggesting you space out," I clarified. "I'm suggesting you discover the aware presence that can make clear, compassionate decisions without being contracted by fear or ego-driven concerns. The wave can navigate its particular circumstances with all the intelligence and power of the ocean behind it."

Over the following weeks, Marcus started exploring what he called "conscious leadership"—making business decisions from a state of aware presence instead of from survival-driven thinking. The results surprised him.

"I had to have a talk with an employee about performance issues," he reported after a particularly challenging week. "Instead of approaching it from my usual anxiety about conflict, I first connected with Loving Awareness. I could feel this vast, spacious presence that included both my care for the company and my care for this person.

"The conversation was honest and direct, but there was an uncommon sense of warmth I haven't felt in these situations before. We came up with solutions I wouldn't have thought of using my usual problem-solving methods. It was as if awareness's intelligence was guiding the conversation."

This was Marcus's first experience of what it means to be both wave and ocean—fully involved in his personal and professional responsibilities while guided by the wisdom and compassion of universal awareness.

The real test occurred during the company's layoffs. Instead of seeing this as a failure of his spiritual practice, Marcus viewed it as a chance to embody Loving Awareness in one of the toughest situations a leader encounters.

"I spent the morning in meditation," he explained, "but not trying to escape what needed to happen. I was asking awareness itself:

'How does care express itself in this situation? What does love look like when difficult decisions are necessary?'"

Marcus was able to make the necessary business decisions while genuinely caring for each affected employee. He personally met with everyone being laid off, offering not only generous severance packages but also his genuine presence to acknowledge their disappointment and concern.

"It wasn't that I enjoyed it or pretended it was pleasant," he reflected. "But I could keep both the business necessity and the human impact in the larger space of awareness. I was fully Marcus the CEO making tough decisions, and at the same time, I was the awareness that could hold everyone involved with compassion."

Several employees later told Marcus that although losing their jobs was tough, his presence and genuine care in handling the situation had actually been healing. Some said they felt more respected and acknowledged in that difficult conversation than they had in years of work elsewhere.

"I realized that trying to transcend my role as CEO was actually a form of spiritual bypassing," Marcus reflected months later. "My awakening isn't separate from my business responsibilities—it's about discovering how Loving Awareness manifests through leadership, through tough decisions, through caring for employees, shareholders, and the broader community we serve."

Six months after learning the ocean and wave teaching, Marcus described a fundamental shift in how he experienced daily life. "I don't switch between being spiritual and being a businessman anymore. It's all one life, all expressions of the same aware presence. When I'm in board meetings, I'm ocean expressing as wave-Marcus navigating corporate challenges. When I'm in meditation, I'm wave-Marcus dissolving back into oceanic awareness. Both are equally sacred."

Marcus realized what contemplatives throughout history have known: we don't need to escape our human lives to embody Loving Awareness. Instead, we can see our human experiences as the very expression of awareness itself—healing from spiritual homesickness by understanding that we never left our true home.

As we heal our own spiritual homesickness by understanding the ocean and wave symbolism, we naturally become a source of healing for others facing the same false choice between a spiritual and worldly life. Marcus's integration allowed him to serve his company and community from a place of genuine wisdom and care rather than spiritual bypassing.

Understanding Non-Duality: Beyond Either/Or

Marcus's journey demonstrates the deep shift from dualistic thinking (either personal or universal, either human or divine, either worldly or spiritual) to non-dual awareness (both/and, or more precisely, neither separate nor identical). This shift is crucial for healing spiritual homesickness because it shows that we have never truly left our true home—we simply were not taught to see our ordinary experience as sacred.

Being Water, Not Just Waves

Spiritual teacher Thich Nhat Hanh often used the metaphor of the ocean and waves to describe our true nature. He would say, "A wave on the ocean has a beginning and an end, a birth and a death. But the wave is empty—full of water, but empty of a separate self."

If a wave only perceives its form, with its rise and fall, it will fear birth and death. But if the wave realizes that it is water and identifies with that water, it will be freed from this fear. The waves come and go, but the water remains unchanged by their passing.

This powerful metaphor helps us understand the unity of form and formlessness. Both the ocean and waves are one substance—water. In their deepest essence, they lack solidity or separation. When we see ourselves and our experiences as temporarily arising and dissolving in the vast ocean of becoming, everything shifts. If we identify solely as individual waves with separate lives, we naturally fear death. However, understanding ourselves as water frees us from this fear because we recognize that water neither begins nor ends.

Beyond Separateness

This is what Loch Kelly calls "Awake Awareness Energy," and what contemplative traditions refer to as dependent co-arising or "one taste"—the union of emptiness and appearance. We become aware of awareness, and from awareness, energy flows, revealing our true interdependence and interconnectedness.

The ocean-wave metaphor demonstrates non-duality, which can be hard to grasp intellectually. The ocean is vast and endless, similar to the field of awareness. A wave rises briefly and then merges back into the water, symbolizing our fleeting moments of awareness. Although these may seem different, both represent awareness, just as an ocean and a wave are both water. Awareness, whether in its temporary wave form or its expansive ocean-like form, is non-dual.

Modern quantum physics presents a similar view. Scientists now propose that all space and matter are made of energy existing at different densities. Energy flows from space into the universe in various forms and processes, then ultimately returns to space. If this truly reflects reality, our sense of duality is fundamentally mistaken.

However, we need to be compassionate with ourselves. Since we were tiny, we have been taught to see ourselves as separate, possibly needing to defend ourselves against the world around us. It takes time to get used to feeling the deep ground of being as always present, and at the same time, to experience and honor the vulnerability of our human experience.

We sometimes describe manifest (coarse) reality and unmanifest (subtle) reality as "foreground" and "background." Although this distinction is not ultimately real, it serves as a helpful teaching tool. The foreground of manifest reality often dominates our consciousness because coarse phenomena tend to be loud, colorful, and attention-grabbing. Meanwhile, subtle awareness stays quietly in the background, easily overlooked unless we intentionally seek it.

However, this analogy has limitations. "One taste" means understanding that all phenomena, internal and external, share a fundamental nature that is luminous and inseparable. This realization goes beyond dualistic views of foreground and background, subject and object, self and other, showing the unified nature of all phenomena.

In contemplative philosophy, the perceived background field is called the knowing part of awareness, while the perceived foreground phenomena represent the lively, expressed part of awareness. The background field is invisible, contentless, formless, boundless, timeless, loving and intelligent. The Dalai Lama refers to it as the "field of benevolence," which matches my experience of its loving nature.

The dynamically expressed aspect encompasses all forms—phenomena, events, and actions. We can learn to shift our awareness between background and foreground, subtle and coarse, unmanifest and manifest dimensions, which are indivisible and co-arising. This is how we could understand non-duality

Non-Dual Recognition

- **Spiritual and Worldly:** All experience occurs within awareness; nothing is outside the sacred
- **Sacred and Ordinary:** Every moment is equally an expression of sacredness
- **Personal and Universal:** Individual expression and Loving Awareness arise together
- **Relative and Absolute:** Conventional and ultimate reality are two sides of one coin
- **Form and Emptiness:** Our humanity is the very expression of our sacred nature

However, these insights need to be integrated gradually and patiently. One moment, we have a deep insight; the next moment, that same insight seems far away. Slowly, but surely, insights about the nature of being visit us more frequently. Often, especially towards the end of life, the veil between personal and ultimate reality becomes almost transparent.

Two Ways of Seeing One Reality: The Personal and Universal Dance

As we wake up from the illusion of separateness and recognize Loving Awareness, we clearly see that everything is interconnected and dependent on each other. This shift in consciousness changes our sense of self. For me, this meant realizing that my "Radhule-ness" was just a fleeting idea, not my true self. I am not a constant, separate, independently existing being, but what Thich Nhat Hanh calls an "interbeing." As poet Mark Nepo writes, we are not "gods who carve out rivers, but particles awakened in the stream."

This insight has significant consequences. As we understand non-duality, our perspective shifts from just ego-driven "prefrontal cortex thinking" to a deeper, broader, and more intuitive way of being. This allows us to become more open-hearted, open-minded, and in harmony with life, even during trying times. This might explain the remarkable resilience shown by Tibetan monks and refugees who have faced great trauma.

Understanding non-duality goes beyond personal spiritual growth. It is essential for tackling our planetary survival crisis because the future of complex life hinges on recognizing our interconnectedness with all living beings. As we face increasing climate change, refugee issues, conflicts, and declining democracies, we need to find new, less divided, and more inclusive ways of seeing and interacting with our world.

The Water Teaching: One Essence, Infinite Expressions

The metaphor of water expressing itself as ocean and waves offers a perfect illustration of non-dual understanding:

Ocean Qualities

- Vast and boundless
- Deep and mysterious
- Timeless and unchanging in essence

- Source of all waves
- Beyond individual characteristics

Wave Qualities

- Distinctive in form and motion
- Temporary and ever-changing
- Interacting with other waves
- Unique personal expression
- Distinct characteristics and patterns

The Non-Dual Truth

Wave and ocean are not separate—they are both water. The wave doesn't need to stop being a wave to be ocean, and the ocean doesn't lose its oceanic nature when it appears as waves. They emerge together, moment by moment, as two aspects of one water-reality.

Similarly, your personal experience (thoughts, emotions, roles, relationships) and universal awareness (spacious, knowing, loving presence) are not separate realities competing for your attention. They are two dimensions of a single seamless experience—the wave-like expression and oceanic essence of your true nature. *(On a Personal Note: see below)*[27]

---

[27] ***On a Personal Note:*** *Learning about non-duality and the ocean and wave nature of ground and phenomena was a huge relief for me. It was as if something had clicked that I formerly had not understood. In some odd way, maybe since I was a child, I had this connection to the sacred. In a chilly environment, this other experience had been my anchor and savior. But I did not know how to put words to that experience. I felt most lost when my belief in science and linear thinking during medical school did not allow me to feel the deep ground of being. Two car accidents, and, strangely enough, two hard knocks against my forehead, freed me from the thick iron band that the conceptual mind had wrapped around my forehead for so long. The near-death-experience had given me a taste of freedom.*

Even though I still get lost in phenomena and my own reactivity, something in me always knows that the other reality is not far away—in fact, that it is right here, now.

Practice: Ocean and Wave Meditation / Pointing-Out-Style

(adapted from Daniel P. Brown)

Time needed: 15-20 minutes

Purpose: Experience non-dual awareness as both ground and expression

Preparation

- Find a comfortable seated position
- Allow your body to settle and become still
- Take a few deep, conscious breaths

Opening the Heart

- Allow your heart to open gently for this practice
- Feel the resonance of your heart throughout your entire body
- Notice how awareness naturally rests within your body and heart
- Set your dedication to practicing for the well-being of all
- Invoke your Field of Care, and your longing to become a Field of Care for others
- Invite a sense of trust—in yourself, in life, in whatever forces of good you have confidence in

Releasing the Separate Self

- Feel your body as a unified whole
- Notice how breath moves through you effortlessly, the body breathing by itself
- Recall your sense of personal identity, your individual self
- Search carefully: can you find anything substantial or permanent about this self?

- As you experience the unfindability of a separate self, rest in what remains—spacious, limitless, boundless awareness
- Recognize that you are now operating as awareness itself

Entering the Ocean of Awareness

- Softly open your eyes and relax your gaze into the space ahead
- Perceive the field of awareness within and around you
- Feel its qualities of complete openness, spaciousness, and aliveness
- Allow awareness to do the meditating; surrender to this process
- With soft, relaxed eyes, gaze into this open-awareness space surrounding you
- Mix your awareness with the space around you until the entire field fills with immediacy and aliveness
- Until a space of open awareness fills everything within and around you

Expanding into Boundlessness

- Pour space into space, awareness into awareness
- Feel the field expanding widely and openly on all sides
- Allow it to extend in all directions—to either side, before, behind, above, below
- Let any perceived margins or limits melt away like breath in cold air
- Notice the timeless quality of this space—an unchanging stillness at its core
- See this space as endless and timeless, like a vast ocean
- Allow yourself to merge with and become this endless, limitless ocean until you and the infinite ocean are one

Being Both Ocean and Wave

- As this vast ocean of awareness, observe your own waves

- Observe thoughts, feelings, and sensations as they arise and fade like waves
- See how all phenomena simply arise and pass away without resistance
- Feel the gentle breeze of freedom flowing through this spaciousness
- When thoughts or feelings arise, imagine pouring a stream of light onto them, dissolving them back into the ocean of awareness
- Experience yourself as both ocean and wave—non-dual awareness expressing as sensations, thoughts, feelings, and sounds
- As this vast ocean, feel your limitless, boundless nature

Extending Compassion

- From this vast perspective, recognize how the ocean can hold and include everything
- Feel how all suffering—of humans, animals, the earth—is held within this depth of compassion
- Know that this spacious, limitless, unchanging awareness is always with you
- Rest in this knowing, for the welfare of all beings
- May this practice benefit all beings everywhere, without exception.

Reflection: Feel this practice in your body, heart, and mind.

Practice: Ocean and Wave Glimpse

(adapted from Loch Kelly)

Time needed: 6 minutes

Purpose: Weave the ocean and wave experience into the day

Instructions:

1. Sit comfortably and be aware of your body supported on a chair or cushion.
2. Begin to be aware of your felt sense of breathing at one specific area of your body.
3. Notice the feeling of your body in this area as your breath naturally comes and goes.
4. Now, notice sensations in your whole body as sensations come and go.
5. Now, notice thoughts, like mental sensations, coming and going.
6. Notice your breath again in one area of your body. Notice the feeling and specific location of your breath in your body.
7. Now, be aware of the area you are focusing from. Feel local awareness, unhook from the focusing location, and open up into the space all around. Open to the space that is aware of the location you were focusing from.
8. Open awareness back and out until you are aware of spacious awareness.
9. Now, be aware from spacious awake awareness of the space, your body sensations, and the location of your breathing all at once.
10. Feel that you are aware from the spacious and pervasive awareness that is effortlessly aware of thoughts, feelings, and sensations like a seamless ocean of awareness arising as the waves of your breath and body.

Reflection: Feel this practice in your body, heart, and mind.

"Infinite No-Self" Glimpse Practice

(adapted from Loch Kelly)

Time needed: 6 minutes

Purpose: Weave the ocean and wave experience into daily life

Time needed: 6 min

Instructions:

1. Close your eyes for a moment and let your awareness scan your entire body-mind system from head to toe, searching for a sense of self as either object or subject. Allow awareness to do a quick yet thorough scan.
2. When you don't identify a self that is fixed in one place or viewed from a single perspective, notice how awareness and aliveness are free, unconfined, and seamlessly permeate everything.
3. Notice that the open, empty awareness is aware of itself, by itself, as itself. The awake field is infinitely aware from everywhere, interconnected with everything. The ocean of awareness knows all waves from inside each wave.
4. Feel as if there is no boundary, no center, yet continue to observe without an observer.
5. Notice the emergence of aliveness in your human body from formless awareness moment to moment.
6. Notice the quality of Now, where everything is here all at once.
7. Let everything be as it is, ordinary and free.

Reflection: Feel this practice in your body, heart, and mind.

When we practice this way, we begin to see ourselves as both the ocean and the wave at the same time. By perceiving ourselves as "in" the ocean, we start to see ourselves "as" both the ocean and the wave. Eventually, we engage with everything from the perspective of being both the boundless ground of awareness and the countless phenomena that arise within it.

This is how wise teachers can be so present with each person they meet: they see themselves and others as waves in the same ocean. From this perspective of non-separation, compassion flows naturally and effortlessly. We understand that all beings, the Earth, air, and waters, are interconnected. All suffering becomes part of us; nothing is separate. Being supported by this vast, spacious perspective allows us to extend compassion to all beings, including ourselves.

As you go through your day, try to remember this ocean and wave perspective. Notice how it changes your relationship with your thoughts, feelings, and the people you meet. In those moments when you see your true nature as both ocean and wave, you connect with the core of non-duality—and by doing so, you connect with the core of compassion itself.

Key Insight: You don't have to choose between being your individual self and being universal awareness. You are the place where these two dimensions meet and express as one lived reality.

Practical Applications: Living as Both Wave and Ocean

The ocean and wave understanding transforms how we approach every aspect of daily life in our spiritually homesick world.

In Relationships

Wave Aspect: Fully embrace your unique self, including your individual communication style, emotional patterns, and ways of caring.
Ocean Aspect: Simultaneously rest in the awareness that sees the other person's true nature beyond their personality patterns.
Integration: Love both personally (wave-to-wave) and universally (ocean recognizing itself in another form), creating relationships that are both intimate and spacious.

In Work and Service

Wave Aspect: Use your specific skills, knowledge, and position to contribute effectively to your organization or community

Ocean Aspect: Act from the wisdom and compassion that flow naturally from awareness itself.
Integration: As Marcus discovered, make decisions and take actions that address both practical needs and the highest good, drawing from personal intelligence and universal wisdom.

In Emotional Challenges

Wave Aspect: Fully experience your emotions as your unique human response to circumstances—don't bypass or spiritualize away real feelings.
Ocean Aspect: Hold these emotions within the expansive space of awareness that stays steady and compassionate regardless of emotional weather.
Integration: Feel emotions like the ocean's waves, not issues to fix, so natural healing and wisdom can surface.

In Spiritual Practice

Wave Aspect: Fully commit to practices with your personal effort, discipline, and dedication.
Ocean Aspect: Recognize that the awareness you're seeking is already present as your own nature—let practices become expressions of recognition and remembering rather than achievement.
Integration: Practice becomes a celebration of what you are rather than an attempt to become something different—healing spiritual homesickness by recognizing you're already home

Common Misunderstandings and How to Navigate Them

"If I'm already the ocean, why do I need to practice?"

The wave doesn't aim to become ocean—it's already part of it. But the wave may need to remember its oceanic nature when caught in stormy weather. Practice helps us recognize and stay grounded in what we already are.

"This sounds like spiritual bypassing—avoiding real human issues"

True non-dual understanding includes everything, especially our humanity. Marcus didn't bypass the difficulty of layoffs; he found a way to handle them from both human compassion and transcendent wisdom. The ocean doesn't transcend waves; it expresses as waves.

"I still feel like a separate person most of the time"

This is natural and not a problem. The wave doesn't feel like the whole ocean—it feels like a wave. But now you can recognize that your wave-experience is happening within and as oceanic awareness. The feeling of separation coexists with the recognition of unity.

"How do I know if I'm acting from ego or from awareness?"

Actions from awareness tend to be naturally wise, compassionate, and appropriate to the situation without forced effort. Actions from ego often have a quality of contraction, self-concern, or force. But don't judge either—even ego-driven actions are waves on the ocean of awareness.

"This seems too good to be true—life is still difficult"

The ocean and wave teaching doesn't promise an easy life. Waves can still be turbulent, storms still arise. But now these difficulties are held within the larger context of Loving Awareness, which provides resilience and wisdom that wasn't available when you identified only as a separate wave.

The Evolution of Identity

As the ocean and wave recognition stabilizes, you may notice a fundamental shift in how you experience identity:

Stage 1: Wave Identity

"I am Marcus, the CEO with particular strengths, weaknesses, history, and challenges. My awareness comes and goes depending on circumstances."

Stage 2: Ocean Identity

"I am boundless awareness temporarily forgetting itself as Marcus. The goal is to transcend this limited identity and remain in oceanic states."

Stage 3: Ocean-Wave Identity

"I am awareness expressing itself as Marcus's unique life. Personal experience and universal awareness arise together as one seamless reality. Both wave and ocean are equally sacred expressions of my true nature."

This final stage embodies what contemplatives call "embodied awakening"—not escaping our humanity, but discovering it as the very expression of sacredness. This is the complete healing of spiritual homesickness: realizing that we never truly left home because our ordinary experience has always been our true home manifesting itself.

Waves in Service to Other Waves

One of the most beautiful aspects of understanding the ocean and waves is how it transforms our way of serving others. When we see that all beings are waves on the same ocean of awareness, service becomes not sacrifice but recognition—oceans caring for themselves in all their forms.

Marcus discovered this in his leadership role. His care for employees wasn't just personal compassion but, instead, like the ocean's natural love for all its waves. This understanding made his service more effective because it came from endless oceanic care rather than limited personal resources.

In our spiritually homesick world, this understanding is urgently needed. As we recognize our essential interconnectedness—not just as philosophy but as lived experience—we naturally begin to care for healing our collective spiritual homesickness. We serve not out of obligation but from the understanding that there is ultimately no "other" to serve—only the one ocean expressing love for itself in countless forms.

The Ripple Effects of Recognition

As you stabilize in ocean and wave awareness, you may notice several natural developments. Those changes usually develop gradually and not in a linear fashion. Be patient and kind with yourself.

Effortless Authenticity: You can be fully yourself without self-consciousness because you know your authentic self is awareness expressing uniquely

Fearless Engagement: You can dive into challenging situations because you know the ocean can't be harmed by whatever waves arise

Natural Authority: Your words and actions carry the weight of oceanic wisdom while remaining appropriately human and relatable

Unconditional Acceptance: You can love others fully as they are because you recognize their essential nature as the same ocean expressing differently

Spontaneous Service: You naturally contribute to healing our spiritually homesick world because you recognize others' homesickness as your own ocean's call for love

Freedom from Spiritual Seeking: The exhausting search for enlightenment dissolves because you recognize you already are what you were seeking—healing from spiritual homesickness

Living the Integration

The ultimate fruit of ocean and wave practice is what Marcus discovered: a life where there's no separation between spiritual and ordinary, sacred and mundane, personal and universal. Everything becomes one seamless expression of aware presence—board meetings and meditation, changing diapers and cosmic consciousness, climate activism and inner peace.

This doesn't mean life becomes problem-free, but it means that problems are contained within the vast context of ocean-like awareness. Challenges still arise, but they're waves on your ocean, rather than threats to your survival. Emotions still flow, but they're seen as the ocean's own movements rather than personal problems to fix.

As you continue this recognition, remember that it's not something to accomplish but a state to acknowledge. You don't need to strive to be both wave and ocean—you simply have to realize that this is what you already are, right now, in this very moment.

In the next chapter, we'll explore what happens when this recognition ignites a deep longing—not for something we lack, but for fully embodying what we've always been. This longing, paradoxically, becomes the very path that guides us back home from spiritual homesickness.

CHAPTER 8

The Longing That Reveals Our True Nature

Understanding our nature as both ocean and wave, both boundless awareness and its unique expressions, often sparks a deep longing. Like Marcus experienced in his spiritual journey, this is not nostalgia for something lost but recognition of something that has always been our true home. This longing itself becomes a gateway to even greater recognition—and the ultimate healing of spiritual homesickness.

This practice offers healing for spiritual homesickness by revealing that the very longing we feel is not a sign of something missing, but the soul's recognition of its true nature calling itself home. The deep ache for meaning, connection, and purpose that characterizes spiritual displacement is actually wisdom—our true nature recognizing itself and calling us to full embodiment.

Ethan, a 25-year-old divinity student, had been attending one of my weekly meditation groups for the past year. Sometimes, he dropped by my office to ask for advice on blending his new practices with his Christian faith.

One day, I asked him, "Does the word 'homesickness' bring anything up for you?" He sighed, leaned back, and started sharing the story of his spiritual journey.

Ethan grew up in a deeply devoted Christian family. "Church wasn't just a place we went on Sundays—it was the center of our lives. "My father was a minister who taught us about God's endless love, Christ's sacrifice, and the call to serve. I was raised surrounded by stories of Jesus healing the sick, feeding the hungry, and embracing those society had cast aside."

Ethan continued thoughtfully, "What resonated most with me was always Jesus's radical compassion—his ability to see beyond surface appearances to the divine spark in everyone. But as I got older, I found myself struggling with certain aspects of how my faith was practiced. Some of the rigidity, the emphasis on sin and unworthiness, and the way complex theological questions were sometimes met with 'just believe'—it didn't feel like it honored the expansiveness of what Jesus actually taught."

"So, what happened?" I asked.

"I went to divinity school hoping to gain a deeper, more nuanced understanding," he said. "I studied comparative religion, biblical history, and theology. The academic study of Christianity broadened my perspective on its historical background and development. I found mystical Christian traditions I'd never encountered—people like Meister Eckhart, Julian of Norwich, and Thomas Merton, who spoke of union with God in ways that felt so immediate and experiential."

Ethan shifted in his chair, his eyes lighting up. "Then I took an elective course on Eastern contemplative traditions, almost by chance. I was just finishing a requirement. But when we studied nondual awareness practices, something resonated deeply. Here were these exact, practical methods for experiencing what the Christian mystics had described—this immediate presence, this ground of being that contains and transcends everything."

He paused, looking troubled for a moment. "At first, I felt guilty, like I was betraying my tradition. I worried about what my father would think. But the more I practiced, the more I realized these approaches weren't taking me away from Christ's teachings—they were giving me tools to experience their essence more directly."

"That's when I found your meditation group," he continued. "I remember the first time you guided us through resting in awareness. It felt like coming home to a place I had always known but somehow forgotten. There was a sense of recognition—not of something new, but of something that had always been here."

Ethan's experience illustrates the spiritual homesickness many young people raised in religious traditions feel as they seek a more direct, personal connection to the divine. His journey demonstrates that this longing isn't a rejection of faith but a deeper quest for the living presence behind religious practices.

"And how do you hold both traditions now?" I asked.

"It's still evolving, then," Ethan admitted. "But I've realized that when Jesus talked about the Kingdom of Heaven being within, or when he said 'I and the Father are one,' he was pointing to this same non-dual reality. The language may differ, but the core idea remains the same."

He continued more confidently. "What's been most transformative is how these practices have deepened my understanding of service. Jesus always emphasized that love of God and love of neighbor are inseparable. But before, my service often came from a place of effort and separation—me helping them. There was a subtle spiritual pride in it."

"And now?" I prompted.

"Now I'm starting to experience service from a place of interconnectedness. When Jesus washed his disciples' feet, he wasn't doing charity—he was showing that we are all part of one body," Ethan explained. "When I rest in awareness before visiting the homeless shelter where I volunteer, something shifts. I'm not bringing Christ's love as something separate. I'm recognizing the Christ consciousness, the aware presence that's already there in each interaction."

Ethan's face softened as he continued. "Last month, I was sitting with a man who's been living on the streets for years. Before, I might have approached him with sympathy or even pity. But that day, after practicing awareness, I could see him with different eyes. There was still compassion, but it came from recognition rather than separation. We shared a meal, and in that simple act, there was a mutual dignity that felt like what Jesus was really teaching."

I nodded, recognizing how effectively he had unified these seemingly different paths.

Ethan reflected, "The Christian tradition speaks of being 'born again.' I used to think this meant simply accepting certain beliefs. But now I see it as what happens when we die to our separate sense of self and awaken to our true nature in God. It's not about believing the right things—it's about experiencing this fundamental shift in identity and perception."

His eyes grew thoughtful. "You know what's beautiful? When I talk with my father about these experiences—carefully, using language he's comfortable with—he recognizes the authenticity. He may not meditate like I do, but he's had moments of grace, moments of disappearing into service, where the same non-dual awareness spontaneously arose."

"That sounds like a real meeting between you and him," I said.

"It is," Ethan agreed. "And it has helped me realize that these contemplative practices aren't about replacing my Christian path but about discovering its true essence. Jesus said, 'I have come that they may have life, and have it abundantly.' That abundance isn't about material wealth—it's about this boundless awareness that encompasses everything."

As our session came to an end, Ethan shared one last insight: "What I'm discovering is that my spiritual homesickness wasn't about needing to leave Christianity or find some exotic alternative. It was a longing for a direct experience of what all the teachings point toward. Both traditions offer different languages and methods for the same homecoming."

Ethan's journey revealed how the longing for our true home goes beyond all traditions—and how spiritual homesickness is ultimately homesickness for the sacred presence that is our deepest nature. In Loving Awareness, he found a place to rest and heal his spiritual wounds, blending the compassionate service at the core of Jesus's teachings with the direct experience of non-dual awareness.

As we heal our own spiritual homesickness by recognizing our longing as wisdom, we naturally become sources of healing for others who experience similar spiritual displacement across all faiths and secular paths.

About Longing for Home

We all share a longing for our true home—a deep sense that the spiritual homesickness so common today points to something vital missing from our lives. All religions and spiritual paths speak of a yearning for something "more" than our everyday reality, calling it by many names—the mystical, the numinous, the sacred, the holy, the Divine, the Sacred Heart, the Great Mystery. In contemplative traditions, this is seen as our true nature, our real self, our essential being. In the Christian tradition, it appears as the "Kingdom of

Heaven within" or what mystics like Meister Eckhart called the "Ground of Being," where the soul and God are one.

In systematic contemplative teachings, realizing our essential nature—the coming together of what we previously described as our personal and universal reality—is sometimes called the "union of mother-consciousness with child-consciousness." When we go, as the Heart Sutra tells us, beyond thought, beyond a personal sense of self, beyond time, and beyond individual consciousness, we are no longer alone. We find ourselves as part of an interconnected and interdependent whole, a dynamic web of being, indivisible links in the fabric of life.

When we release our individual sense of self and step into the realm of Loving Awareness, a profound shift occurs. The Christian mystic Thomas Merton describes this beautifully: this "surrender to a power of love that is greater than human [helps us] to move toward God in a darkness that surpasses the light of reason and human understanding." He explains the transition into what Loch Kelly calls "open-hearted awareness," John Makransky refers to as a "Field of Care," Daniel P. Brown named "Rigpa," and Joanna Macy described at a dinner with a bright smile, "The Immensity." Once again, in Merton's words, we arrive at the "loving, unitive and supernatural love of God that is beyond concepts." Recognizing that such experiences are hard to fully understand and that we are attempting to express what cannot truly be put into words, he adds, "The transcendent experience of God in love is felt as a knowing of unknowing, and a seeing that is not seeing."

Loch describes the transition from the conceptual mind to Loving Awareness as a "not knowing that knows." Paradoxically, the "not knowing" of Loving Awareness is the highest form of certainty available to us. Our experiences of depth push us beyond our thinking mind.

When we let go of the conceptual mind, when past, present, and future merge into the present, and when there is no inside and no outside, we can experience an all-at-once-ness, an all-around-ness—a boundless, groundless ground composed of nothing—just openness and knowingness, emptiness and fullness, and radical, complete effortlessness. As we feel ourselves securely held in this "Field of Benevolence," we find that we are home, completely healing spiritual homesickness.

A word of caution: the experiences we encounter on the spiritual path can be both enjoyable and seductive, potentially leading to dead ends if we're not careful. Teacher Chögyam Trungpa called this "spiritual materialism," where we pursue peak experiences for their own sake, "just to have the experience," as just another stamp in our spiritual collection. Then we become attached to "states" of experience. Spiritual ambition, which sees success as reaching a special state as the ultimate goal of our practice, is an obstacle on the path that can disconnect us from others and the world we live in.

The guiding star on our journey home is what we might call "the holiness of our heart's intention." Our heart's intention acts as the North Star that guides us toward the sacred and Loving Awareness. In the words of the 14th-century mystic who wrote *The Cloud of Unknowing*: "God is incomprehensible to the knowing power but to the loving power, he is, in every man diversely, comprehensible to the full." Thomas Merton adds, "Union with God in love implies a profound existential grasp of His presence. Heart knowing is an experience that is entirely intuitive and not at all intellectual."

John Makransky sees resting in the deepest part of being, the space where we all ultimately connect, as the foundation we need to stay grounded in, from which we relate to life. From there, what contemplatives call "the awakened heart" arises—our strong desire for the well-being and liberation of those in distress. Contributing to alleviating that suffering is seen as the highest purpose of our lives.

In these practices that follow, we experience this union with the sacred as part of Loving Awareness—an open-hearted awareness that lovingly embraces the sea of interconnected beings. We might refer to this, as spiritual teacher Ram Dass does, as Loving Awareness—the ultimate home that heals all spiritual homesickness.

The Geography of Spiritual Homesickness

Before we explore the practices that lead us home, it's helpful to remember once more the landscape of spiritual homesickness in our modern world. This deep longing manifests differently for different people, but common patterns include:

The Achievement Paradox: Many successful people feel a crisis of meaning: Is this all there is? Also, the increasing divide between those who have and those who do not have, leave those who have and are aware, burdened with shame and guilt. They might ask: how can I lead such a lucky life, when so many are left behind?

Digital Displacement: We're more "connected" than any generation in history, yet loneliness and isolation are at epidemic levels. Social media gives the illusion of connection but often makes us feel more separated from real community and meaning. In addition, social media and AI increase polarization and misunderstandings between groups. Instead of interconnectedness, they further separation and misgivings.

Cultural Fragmentation: Racism, division between rich and poor, between secular and religious, between left-leaning and right-leaning have increased. Many feel confused and caught between their families' and friends' beliefs and their own.

Information Overwhelm: Constant exposure to global suffering via news and social media can cause a numbing disconnect as a defense. This numbing effect conflicts with our natural empathy. Through practice, compassion and interbeing become stronger. We might feel helpless and too vulnerable as our hearts break.

Environmental Grief: Increasing awareness of ecological destruction fosters a deep sense of disconnection from our natural home. We might feel a sense of powerlessness and grief as we see our country care less and less about global warming, rising sea levels, and the plight of poor countries affected by the climate crisis. We feel homesick not only for personal meaning but also for our place within the web of life. Deep in our body, in our unconscious, many sense that something is wrong. Instead of contracting and shutting down, getting rooted deeply in the field of Loving Awareness helps us to stay present, openhearted, and engaged on behalf of our planet.

Again, understanding these patterns shows that spiritual homesickness isn't a personal failure but a natural response to living in a world that has lost its humanity and spiritual essence. Getting rooted deeply in our spiritual home helps us to be a force for good on behalf of ourselves, those around us and our world.

Why Our World Became Spiritually Homesick

Several historical and cultural shifts have contributed to the epidemic of spiritual homesickness in our time.

The Industrial Revolution's Legacy: The shift from an agrarian to an industrial society separated us from natural rhythms and cycles, replacing awareness of seasons with clock time, and community interdependence with individual competition. Racism, increased through slavery, workers are used for cheap labor, capitalism leads to a new aristocracy of billionaires.

Scientific Materialism: Although scientific advances have delivered great benefits, the sole focus on material reality has left many feeling spiritually hungry. Many are searching for meaning in a worldview that accepts only what is "evidence-based" and ignores the sacred dimension of existence.

Consumer Culture's False Promises: We've been conditioned to seek fulfillment through physical possessions—buying the right products, gaining the right status, accumulating the right experiences. Inner fullness and connection to the web of life have been neglected. Recognizing the wholeness and belonging that is already present gives us the strength to resist those who gain from exploitive capitalism and autocracy.

Loss of Initiation and Ritual: Traditional cultures offered clear paths for spiritual growth through rites of passage and communal ceremonies. Modern society provides few meaningful ways to recognize spiritual transitions or connect with community, the web of life, and transcendental reality. We need to teach our kids and the next generation that living with an open heart for the common good is important and essential to creating our future world.

Re-envisioning Globalization as Going Beyond Self-Interest: Turning alienation and separation into a universal sense of generosity that transcends tribal ties would foster greater willingness to share and keep our hearts open. Global generosity and tolerance could be a foundation for peace.

Recognizing these larger patterns helps us see that healing spiritual homesickness isn't just an individual effort but a collective need for spiritual renewal today.

Practices to Help Us Come Home to Awareness

Pointing-Out-Style Practices

Before introducing the following practices, I want to clarify what we mean by "holding the view," as understanding this concept is important. "To hold a view" is a combination of attitude and perspective. It means maintaining a specific inner viewpoint with stability, steadiness, openness, and ease.

Each new perspective builds on the previous ones, much like a widening spiral includes all its earlier turns. These different viewpoints help us see Loving Awareness more clearly and deeply. We notice Loving Awareness in its qualities of spaciousness, clarity, and immediacy. We experience it as timeless, vast, and boundless, realizing that everything is insubstantial or "empty." Then we arrive at the view of non-duality and understand that there is "no inside and no outside." The wave is the ocean, and the ocean is the wave. Loving Awareness and phenomena are one and the same, just as ocean and wave are both water. All is Loving Awareness, whether it's spacious, formless, and knowing, or arising as lively energy and form. We then reach the view of awareness turning inward. With this, a major shift happens from a localized sense of self to a boundless one, and our hearts open wide, like a blooming lotus—fully healing spiritual homesickness.

PRACTICE: Awareness Turning Toward Itself

(Lion's Gaze—adapted from Daniel P. Brown)

Time Needed: 15-20 minutes

Purpose: To transition from separate self to unity with Loving Awareness—this practice offers healing for spiritual homesickness by revealing that what longs for home is itself the home we seek

Instructions:

1. **Establish a strong foundation**
   - Settle into your body's sensations
   - Feel solid like a mountain
   - Keep your back strong and heart open

2. **Set your intention**
   - Awaken so you can work for the welfare of all beings
   - Invite the support and protection of everything good
   - Feel this resonance in your heart

3. **Practice emptiness of self**
   - Using high-speed awareness, search for a solid sense of self
   - When it recedes as unfindable, affirm what remains
   - Experience this open, spacious field of awareness

4. **Connect from the centerless center**

- See the field of awareness as your true center
- Recognize it as the "centerless center" from which you connect to life

5. **Open to boundless space**
    - Open your eyes and look into the open awareness space before you
    - Pour your awareness into awareness, until only open awareness space remains

6. **Dissolve all boundaries**
    - If you meet edges, open into them
    - Watch as these boundaries dissolve
    - Experience how only openness remains

7. **Become ocean watching waves**
    - Feel yourself as the ocean of awareness
    - Watch phenomena arising and falling like waves
    - See all waves as insubstantial
    - Recognize them as dynamic events coming into being and dissolving

8. **Experience non-duality**
    - Know ocean and waves are indivisible, non-dual, like sun and its rays, or the moon and its glow
    - There is a single non-dual field of awareness—no inside, no outside
    - Be clear and open like the sky

9. **Dissolve all arising phenomena**
    - Notice when thoughts, feelings, sounds, or other phenomena arise
    - Pour the crystal-clear water of awareness into them
    - Watch them dissolve until only the field of awareness is present

10. Rest in effortlessness

- Feel the sense of aliveness and effortlessness, like a warm, gently falling rain
- You don't have to do or fix anything—just let the rain fall, all by itself

11. Experience the luminous heart

- Your heart feels bright and lucid, natural and simple
- Be this vast, non-dual awareness as it radiates out in all directions

12. Turn awareness towards itself

- Now, turn awareness towards its own openness and limitlessness
- Notice how your heart opens wider still

13. Rest and radiate

- Rest in this wide openness, this brightness, softness, and care
- Like the sun, radiate this awakeness, this lucidity, warmth, and presence
- Feel gratitude having found home, for the welfare of all beings

Reflection: Feel this practice in your body, heart, and mind.

(On a Personal Note: see below)[28]

---

[28] ***On a Personal Note:*** *"Lion's Gaze" or "Turning Awareness onto itself" has been the practice that allows me most to experience the space and wisdom qualities of Loving Awareness. The qualities of love and surrender are stronger, in my experience, when the spacious quality is there first.*

As a disclaimer, for others this might be the other way around, or this might be dependent on the day you practice.

"Lion's Gaze" opens up Awake Loving Awareness to all sides, as if blasting open a space of light energy. With this experience, which also goes along with a profound sense of emptiness of self, I can go beyond myself

Practice: Field of Awake Loving Awareness

Time Needed: 15-20 minutes

Purpose: To connect with the loving quality of awareness—mending the ache in your heart by realizing that our longing for love is the love of awareness recognizing itself

Instructions:

1. **Begin with body awareness**
   - Feel the sensations in your body
   - Experience your body as a whole
   - Feel your body as an energy field
   - Notice its impermanent, constantly changing nature

2. **Open to breath and surroundings**
   - Feel how your whole body is breathing
   - Don't block anything out—thoughts or sounds
   - Don't follow them either
   - Allow your whole body to fill with awareness
   - Feel the space around you

3. **Connect with the field of loving care**
   - Imagine the space around you as a field of loving care
   - Remember a caring moment with another person, someone you feel connected to, someone who is with you in a deep way
   - Feel their happiness for your well-being

4. **Evoke the feeling of connection**
   - Feel being with this person now, this being who means you well

---

and just be open. I love it. From there, I can then more easily feel the warmth and love incited by the following practices.

- Consider not only other people, but spiritual figures like Christ, Mary, Moses, Allah, or a wisdom figure, or something in nature like a tree, or the Great Mystery

5. **Expand into the field of awareness**
   - Let the memory go, yet feel deeply the felt sense of that experience
   - Widen this felt sense of loving care into the field of awareness
   - Feel it steeped in loving energy

6. **Include all feelings**
   - If you notice anxiety, let it be held in this field
   - Allow these tender qualities into your body and mind
   - Let every part of you be loved in its very being
   - Accept any worries or fears
   - Allow them to be held in love

7. **Embrace all mind states**
   - If your mind wanders, accept it, embrace it
   - Let the field of love and care settle into you
   - If there is hesitancy or self-criticism, allow and embrace these too
   - Rest back into this loving field

8. **Extend to all beings**
   - Imagine this loving energy shining through you
   - Send the energy out to others, to all beings
   - Relax deeply into this field
   - Wish deeply for all beings to be well
   - Hold the wish to relieve their suffering

9. **Rest in openness**
   - Let heart and mind fall completely open, as if falling into space
   - Let everything be just as it is

10. Reorient as needed

- Orient your awareness towards the Field of Care
- Feel your body and breath
- If distracted, invoke this field of loving care, again and again

11. Personalize your practice

- Make this practice your own
- See what your Heart-Mind needs today

12. Return and dedicate

- Come back to the body
- Dedicate the merits of this meditation to all beings

Reflection: Feel this practice in your body, heart, and mind.

(On a Personal Note: see below)[29]

---

[29] ***On a Personal Note:*** *After "Lion's Gaze" allowed the space of light, awakeness, and wisdom to open for me, with the "Field of Awake Loving Awareness" practice, warmth, gentleness and love can now flood in. I feel the Field of Care more strongly when the spacious quality has been opened first. For me it is as if the love and warmth-quality appears now within a ground of energy and light. This strong experience helps me to leave my small self behind, and merge with universal self.*

Recently I had a difficult day with a client of mine not doing well. I felt responsible and that I should have "fixed" her suffering. Doing this practice allowed me to go beyond my small therapist self, and experience a balance that is a priori there. That experience of knowing, ease, and love allowed me to see myself with more compassion and wisdom. It strangely also allowed the relationship between my client and myself to unfold in a healing way.

Finding Our True Home by Surrendering to the Mystery

We find our way home by connecting to the Great Mystery, the Ground of Being, the Field of Loving Awareness. This is a gradual process: first, we get a taste of it, then we allow ourselves to consider that this might be real. Later on, we discover a path there. By practicing this path repeatedly, a strong cord of connection naturally develops.

The next step goes beyond connection. John Makransky teaches us: "Allow the body sense of feeling to draw you into oneness with it"; "Allow breath to draw you into oneness with it"; and "Allow awareness and space to draw you into oneness with it." At the heart of each of these steps is surrender—a letting go of control, a stepping away from the ego's rule.

We allow boundless openness and awareness to draw us into itself. If you offer yourself up to "something," it can be personal, like God, or impersonal, such as loving knowing awareness. Yet, the Great Mystery is not something, "a thing," or a "someone" that can be reified. Now, we are entering unfamiliar territory, which asks us to trust and let go into not knowing, beyond intellectual understanding.

Practice: Completely Surrender to your Spiritual Home

(adapted from John Makransky)

Time Needed: 15-20 minutes

Purpose: To connect with the loving quality of awareness—healing spiritual homesickness by recognizing that our longing for love is the love of awareness recognizing itself.

Instructions:

1. **Begin with body awareness**
   - Feel the sensations in your body
   - As awareness shifts from the thinking mind into the body as a whole, feel your body as an alive field of energy
   - Sense its impermanent, constantly changing nature

2. **Open to breath and surroundings**
   - Feel your whole body breathe
   - Don't block anything out—thoughts, sounds, sensations
   - Don't follow them either
   - While your whole body fills with awareness, sense the edges and boundaries as open—no inside, no outside

3. **Connect with the field of loving care**
   - Imagine the space around you as a field of loving care
   - Remember the experience of a spiritual Field of Care
   - Evoke whatever or whoever is most powerful for you—happy for your well-being, wishing you well, completely unconditional and unchanging

4. **Evoke the feeling of connection**
   - Feel that this is really happening—you are seen, held in unconditional love and wisdom
   - Accept the connection, just allow it
   - Surrender your struggle
   - Feel the tender qualities infusing you and all beings, your whole world
   - Let these qualities and energies draw you down into their source, into complete depth

5. **Allow the wish to surrender**
   - Let a strong wish arise for you to offer yourself up to the source of these energies
   - Surrender to the depth of all being, to the sacred
   - Whatever quality that has for you, let that strong wish, as it wells up, become radiance emanating from your heart,

just like a rainbow that transforms everything into luminous offerings

- Sense that as truly happening

6. **Expand into the field of awareness**
    - Let the rainbow offering become a deeply felt sense of that experience
    - Imagine your offering as joyfully received by these energies
    - Let more and more radiance from your heart continue to radiate out and become luminous offerings that are received and absorbed completely, offered up to their deepest nature that is one with yours

7. **Include all feelings**
    - Now imagine that all your emotions and reactions as you bring them to mind have transformed into rainbow radiance from your heart
    - All emotions and reactions that you had or will have become spontaneously offered as rainbow radiance from your heart
    - Anxiety, worry, anger, love—let them become radiance-offerings from your core

8. **All becoming radiance offerings**
    - All phenomena like rainbows from your heart, offer them up to the true nature of our being
    - As your thoughts, feelings, and perceptions are arising, let them be offered up to the sacred figures, the deepest depth, the great mystery
    - Imagine them dissolving deeply into this radiance, absorbed into total one-ness with the sacred figures, the great mystery

9. **Rest in openness as a unified field of everything**
    - Relax and dissolve into the great oneness
    - Let heart and mind fall open

- Experience a unity of space and awareness that pervades all, as if falling into space—a pervasive openness like a sunlit shy
- Let everything just be as it is

10. Finding home

- Absorb thoughts and feelings that arise into their natural source, dissolved into the luminous ground of being
- Be one with your original Field of Care
- Rest into just being one with home

Reflection: Feel this practice in your body, heart, and mind

Try this practice, and see what happens. Notice any discomfort or a maybe sense of relief. Or, this might be an experience you have known all along, but you didn't realize that you knew it experientially. You might even like to sit down and journal a bit. *(On a Personal Note: see below)*[30]

---

[30] ***On a Personal Note:*** *John Makransky's practice "How to Completely Surrender to My Spiritual Home" has become the most important practice for me these days. Even though, as a post Catholic with some resistance to authority, the idea of surrender was at first strange to me, this has become the practice where I can most let go of my ego-self, my sense of control, my opinions of how things should be done. In a way, this practice has become for me an alternative "emptiness of self" practice. As my controlling self "empties out," the sacred can come in. This practice allows me to be most open to the Numinous," the great Mystery, the groundless ground. As the sacred fills the space within and around me, there is complete quiet, ease, awakeness, warmth, and, yes, love. I am reminded of the St. Francis Prayer: "Make me an instrument of your peace." In my experience, I can be the most useful, when I am engaged from that level of surrender.*

I realize that for me there is a sequence. First there is an emphasis on light and wisdom with "Lion's Gaze," the follows warmth and love with "The Field of Awake Loving Awareness," culminating in "How to Completely Surrender to my Spiritual Home" with a complete unity with the sacred. The sequence might be different for you, but you can try this and tell me how this works.

In Ethan's journey, as in yours, the longing for home is fulfilled when we experience the sacred as something alive and real. It also helps to understand that many different spiritual traditions point to the same universal truth. By combining the wisdom of contemplative practices with our personal beliefs, we find that the home we've been searching for has always been here—in the vast awareness that is our true nature, in the loving heart that recognizes our deep connection with all beings, and in the compassionate service that naturally flows from this understanding.

This recognition offers essential healing for spiritual homesickness. We understand that we have never truly been homeless—we just looked in the wrong places. Our true home isn't a physical location or even perfect life circumstances. It is the aware, loving presence that we are, that we have always been, and that we can never really lose.

"That is full, this is full,
From that fullness comes this fullness,
If you take away this fullness from that fullness,
Only fullness remains."

-Invocatory verse of Isha Upanishad

PART III

LOVE IN ACTION—WHEN HEALING BECOMES SERVICE

QR Code for the Audio for Practices in Part III

or visit https://www.radhuleweiningerphd.com/spiritual-homesick-ness-part-three

CHAPTER 9

When Pain Becomes a Gateway to Compassion

In Part II, we learned to recognize and rest in Loving Awareness with greater stability. We learned to connect with it, relate to it, and even surrender to it at times. We now understand that we are not separate from this awareness; we are its very expression. The next important step is integration: How do we live from this understanding? How do we approach our relationships, work, and the world's challenges from this deeper foundation?

Part III explores what I call "Engaged Awareness"—not spiritual bypassing or detaching from life's challenges, but a deeper, compassionate, and wise involvement with everything we face. When Loving Awareness awakens to itself, our heart naturally opens, and our desire to serve appears spontaneously.

Returning home to Loving Awareness is deeply healing, but it doesn't remove life's unavoidable challenges. In fact, as our hearts open more fully, we might feel the world's pain more intensely—including the collective pain of spiritual homesickness that affects so many in our disconnected world. How can we stay open without becoming overwhelmed? How can we allow our toughest emotions to become gateways to even greater compassion? This is where our practice genuinely takes courage.

This practice offers healing for spiritual homesickness by transforming personal crises into a healing presence for others. When we learn to be compassionately present with our own pain, we naturally develop the capacity to hold space for others experiencing their own forms of spiritual displacement—completing the triple medicine by providing meaningful service that flows from love.

Mark's Story: From Crisis to Compassion

I first met Mark at one of my weekly meditation classes at the community center. He struck me as someone who approached practice with earnest dedication, always sitting near the front, his questions thoughtful and precise. A software developer in his late forties, he had initially come seeking techniques to manage work stress, but something in him clearly hungered for deeper understanding.

When he arrived at my office for our scheduled session that afternoon, I immediately noticed the change. His normally composed demeanor had shifted to something raw and unsettled. His shoulders were hunched, his eyes downcast as he sank into the chair across from me.

"I lost my job this morning," he said, his voice barely above a whisper. "Twenty years of experience, gone in an email. A company-wide layoff." He looked up, and I could see the fear swimming in his eyes. "I have two teenagers, college around the corner, a mortgage... my wife's teaching salary won't come close to covering it all."

Mark's crisis wasn't just about unemployment—it was about the collapse of the identity and security that many use to avoid confronting deeper spiritual homesickness. When our external structures crumble, we're often forced to face the fundamental questions about meaning and identity that we've been avoiding.

I nodded, giving him space for his words to fully land. "What are you feeling in your body right now, Mark?" I asked gently.

He placed a hand on his chest. "It's tight here, like I can't breathe properly. And my stomach feels hollow." His voice caught. "But what's worse is the shame. How do I tell my family that I can't provide for them anymore? What does that make me?"

I saw this moment as a crucial turning point. Mark stood at a threshold that pain unexpectedly revealed before him. He could either avoid it through denial, distraction, or drowning in it, or he could face it with compassionate awareness. That's exactly why I introduced the practice of compassionate presence to feelings in our previous sessions.

"Mark," I said, "would you be willing to work with these feelings using the practice we've been developing?"

He nodded, straightening slightly in his chair.

The Four-Step Practice in Action

"Let's start by simply observing what's coming up," I guided. "Can you name the feelings you're feeling?"

"Fear," he said immediately. "Shame. Confusion. Anger, too, I think."

"Good," I affirmed. "Now, for the second step, can you allow these feelings to take up all the space they need? Instead of trying to make them smaller or push them away, give them room to breathe and find their own place."

I watched as Mark closed his eyes, and his breathing deepened. The tension on his face stayed, but something around it was softening.

"Now rest with or within these feelings," I continued. "Not trying to change them, just being with them fully."

We sat in silence for several minutes. I noticed the subtle changes in his expression—moments of intensity followed by slight releases, the natural unfolding that occurs when we create a compassionate space for our pain.

"And finally," I said softly, "allow everything to be, with spaciousness. Nothing to fix, nothing to change."

When Mark finally opened his eyes, I saw what I've witnessed countless times in my work—that unmistakable shift when someone realizes they are bigger than their pain. The feelings hadn't gone away, but they had found their proper place within his awareness rather than consuming it completely.

"It's still there," he said with mild surprise, "all of it. But it's not... drowning me anymore. It's like I found a place to stand."

"That's exactly it."

The Ripple Effects

In our upcoming sessions, Mark shared how this practice helped him get through the tough weeks of unemployment. He talked about telling his family about losing his job that evening, and how staying present with his fear and shame—rather than being overwhelmed by them—allowed him to remain steady. His wife and teenage children responded with support instead of the disappointment he had feared.

What touched me most was how Mark started to use this practice not just for himself but to help others. He shared how he sat with his brother, who had received a difficult health diagnosis, guiding him through the same four steps: noticing the feelings, allowing them space, resting with them, and letting everything be.

"I never expected this," Mark said during one of our later sessions, now three months into his unemployment. "I started meditating to be less stressed at work, and now I don't even have a job. But I've found something I never would have discovered otherwise."

"What's that?" I asked.

"That my suffering can serve as a doorway rather than just a dead end. When I stopped fighting it and learned to be with it compassionately, it revealed parts of myself I never knew existed—my ability to be present not only with my own pain but also with others."

Mark eventually found a new job that allowed him more flexibility to be with his family. But what he gained during that painful period of uncertainty was far more valuable than just job security. He learned what I hope all my students eventually realize—that our greatest suffering, when faced with compassionate presence, can become our deepest teacher and an unexpected way to serve others—transforming even spiritual homesickness into a path of awakening.

As we heal our own spiritual homesickness through these practices, we naturally become medicine for others suffering the same collective disconnection. Mark's transformation enabled him to serve his family and community from a place of authentic presence rather than desperate striving.

Understanding Pain as a Gateway

When our Feelings become a Doorway to Awareness

Learning to tap into Loving Awareness can be truly beautiful. If you've experienced even glimpses of it, you know what I mean—those moments of spaciousness, clarity, and peace that feel so comforting. I've had meditation experiences that were so profoundly beautiful that I sometimes found myself thinking, "Why work with difficult emotions when I can just rest in this amazing awareness?"

However, I've realized that recognizing and resting in Loving Awareness must include our entire human experience. It should enhance our lives rather than serve as an escape from them. This is what transforms practice into what I call "Awake Loving Awareness."

This is where we need to be careful about what psychologist John Wellwood calls "spiritual bypass"—using spiritual practices to avoid facing our unresolved emotions, sidestepping our wounds, or dodging the messiness of our relationships. It's tempting, isn't it? When we experience those peaceful states during meditation—the bliss, the spaciousness—there's a natural urge to rise above the raw, messy parts of being human.

But if we try to go beyond our human needs and painful emotions before we've fully faced them, something happens: those hurts don't disappear—they hide beneath the surface. And when we're stressed or triggered, they resurface, often with unexpected force.

This is especially important when dealing with spiritual homesickness. Often, the desire for transcendence or "higher states" can become another way of avoiding, where we attempt to escape the core disconnection instead of healing it with compassionate presence.

The Integration of Psychology and Spirituality

In my previous book, *Heart Medicine*, I discussed what I call "LRPPs"—long-standing, recurrent, painful patterns. These resemble what psychologists call "complexes," and in contemplative psychology, they are recognized as unresolved emotional patterns, or seeds, that keep cycling through our experience until we meet them with wisdom and compassion.

Another helpful approach is Internal Family Systems (IFS), developed by Richard Schwartz. IFS sees the mind as made up of different parts or subpersonalities—the manager, the exile, the firefighter. Beneath these parts is your core Self, which we might call Awake Loving Awareness. As my colleague Loch Kelly writes, "The goal isn't to judge, minimize, or get rid of these parts, but to notice and lovingly embrace them all from our interconnected Self."

This is where the integration becomes powerful. When we combine psychological understanding with our awareness practices, we create something meaningful. Our practice helps us access the broader context of awareness, while understanding our psychological patterns allows us to work skillfully with what arises.

Good therapy can be incredibly beneficial in addressing our painful patterns. It provides a safe space where we are seen and understood, helping us feel secure enough to experience our genuine emotions. True healing starts by recognizing and embracing our difficult experiences so we can hold them within Awake Loving Awareness. When we do this, these tough knots of hurt can soften, become fluid, and eventually transform.

The Field of Care as Foundation

When we practice regularly with a method that guides us to experience Loving Awareness, then this pathway becomes ingrained into our way of being. From a Western perspective, we could understand it as a habitual pathway our body will now instinctively follow. Tibetans understand this process as an unclogging of ancient pathways, which then remain open. By remembering and recognizing Loving Awareness as an energy that is already there, we learn to experience this as a Field of Care, as a vast, always present energy that we can rest in and trust to be there as our spiritual ground. *(On a*

Personal Note: see below)[31]

But if we can't access this broader perspective—if we only operate from our limited, separate sense of self—we remain vulnerable to our reactive patterns. When this becomes our default way of experiencing the world, we find ourselves overwhelmed by difficult thoughts, feelings, and worries—including the constant sense of disconnection that characterizes spiritual homesickness.

Loch Kelly describes one trap as falling into a "psychological underpass," where our wounds become our entire identity. Emotions, especially painful ones, can be persistent and convincing. They can persuade us that we are only our wounded selves—just the victim, the failure, or the abandoned one—or, in the case of spiritual homesickness, just the person who doesn't belong anywhere.

There's another common trap he calls the "cognitive overpass"—becoming a "mindful witness" or "rational manager" who tries to keep emotions in check and control life. But unresolved pain often lies beneath this tidy surface. This is just another strategy of the separate self.

The beauty of these practices is that when we open our hearts with awareness, wisdom, and love, these qualities naturally flow into our lives. From this expansive space, our deepest wounds can finally meet the loving wholeness that has always been within us. The tight grip of old hurts begins to loosen. We realize that we are—and have always been—waves in the vast ocean of awareness—never actually separate from our true home.

---

[31] ***On a Personal Note:*** *When I first began opening to Loving Awareness—this sense of vast, Loving Awareness that's always present—I started trusting something greater than my personal will. I experienced a clear sense of knowing, love, and care within awareness itself. As I improved at recognizing this field quality of awareness, moving into it, and resting in it, I saw that these qualities of love and wisdom appeared naturally, without any effort on my part.*

This shift transformed everything. I could now see myself—this specific human being with all my quirks and limitations—from the wide perspective of Loving Awareness. I understood that my true home is John Makransky's Field of Care, where wisdom, love, knowing, and aliveness naturally arise.

Practical Approaches to Pain as a Gateway

The Source of Sustainable Compassion

Something remarkable happens when our compassion flows from an awakened heart rather than obligation or effort: we don't become exhausted. There's no "compassion fatigue" or burnout. Our love and care naturally rise, like clear water from an underground spring that never runs dry.

I've realized that the source of our love, compassion, generosity, and forgiveness isn't something we need to create. It comes from what I sometimes call the "groundless ground"—the vast, limitless, deeply nurturing source that exists within and beyond everything we can imagine.

One of my students, Maria, a nurse in a busy emergency room, described this beautifully: "For years, I thought compassion meant pushing myself to care until I was completely drained. I'd go home empty and wake up dreading my next shift. Now I understand that true compassion comes from a deeper place—not from emptying my cup but from connecting with a flowing river that runs through everything. The difference is profound."

Establishing the Field of Care

When we learn to turn this Field of Care into a real experience rather than just an idea, it becomes a safe foundation for our entire lives. I explored the Field of Care in previous chapters. Now, and especially in Chapter 10, we learn to make the Field of Care a vital part of the foundation of our lives. Whatever challenges we face, we can handle them better when we are grounded in the experience of being held in Loving Awareness.

When the Field of Care becomes a natural part of who we are, we become more resourceful and resilient—for our own benefit and for others. When pain arrives, as it inevitably does, it can strengthen our connection to this deep ground of being rather than overwhelm us—including the pain of spiritual homesickness that affects so many in our disconnected world.

With consistent practice, a hardened ego softens into openness. We become more adaptable, receptive, and open to love—even during challenging times. *(On a Personal Note: see below)*[32]

Core Practices

Practice: Loving Field of Care

(adapted from John Makransky)

Time required: 10-15 minutes

Purpose: To create a solid foundation of Loving Awareness that can hold our pain— this practice offers healing for existential pain and spiritual lostness by establishing a secure base of love from which we can face all experience

---

[32] ***On a Personal Note:*** *The insight that true compassion comes straight from the field of Loving Awareness, the ground of being, came to me gradually. At first, when meeting Sharon Salzberg's book on Loving Kindness in the mid-eighties, I was just relieved that there was warmth and compassion as part of the practice.*

Then I realized that this kindness, compassion, and sympathetic joy came from my good intentions. It seemed conceptual and at times contrived, even though on long retreats the warmth would sink down into my heart. Still, this kind of kindness and compassion seemed exhaustible, and one could burn out despite those good intentions.

When I discovered non-dual practices 25 years ago, I began to realize that warmth and compassion were the qualities of the ground of being, of the field of Loving Awareness. When realized in that way, I, as the experiencer of those qualities, could not burn out. I understood that the qualities of the field of awareness were inexhaustible.

Instructions:

Grounding in Body and Awareness

- Feel the sensations in your body, your body as a whole
- Allow awareness to shift from the thinking mind into the body
- Feel your whole body as awareness, as a field of energy
- Notice its permeable nature, constantly changing
- Feel your body from the inside out
- Let yourself be drawn into its depths

Grounding in Breath

- Feel the sensation of your entire body breathing
- Let thoughts, sounds, and feelings pass through freely
- Experience breath breathing you

Remembering a Moment of Care

- Bring to mind a caring moment with another person, someone you feel connected to, someone who has been with you in a deep way, who wishes you well, who sees you clearly with warmth
- This might be a person you know, a spiritual figure, a wise teacher, the Great Mystery, nature, or a beloved pet

Embodying the Feeling of Care

- Let go of the specific image and stay with the felt sense of warmth and care
- Allow this field of awareness to become steeped in loving energy

Including Difficult Feelings in the Field of Care

- When you notice anxieties or fears, let them be held in this love and care
- If spiritual homesickness arises—that deep longing for meaning and connection—welcome it into this field with the same loving acceptance
- Let these tender qualities fill your body and mind
- Every part of you is loved in its very being
- If worries or fears arise, accept those feelings, allowing them to be held in love
- When your mind wanders, accept it, embrace it
- Let the field of love and care settle into you
- Rest in this loving field

Extending Care Outward

- Imagine this loving energy shining through you to others
- Relax deeply into this field and wish all beings well

Resting in the Field

- Let heart and mind fall fully open, as if into infinite space
- Let everything be just as it is
- Wish all beings well

Reflection: Feel this practice in your body, heart, and mind.

Advanced Integration

When Pain Becomes a Doorway to Awareness

Pain can serve as a direct portal to resting in awareness itself. Here we use emptiness practices to dissolve the rigid patterns that form around hurt or trauma, allowing the fluidity and openness of our true nature to surface.

When we're hurt, our thoughts and emotions can become tangled, tightening the knot of suffering. We often react by grasping for what we want or pushing away what we don't want. This creates more suffering and makes us reactive, leading to blame, dejection, or shame.

The Emptiness of Pain practice below helps free us from these knots of suffering without spiritual bypassing. Instead, it becomes a doorway to open-hearted awareness—transforming even spiritual homesickness into a gateway to recognizing our true nature.

Practice: Emptiness of Pain

Time Needed: 15-20 minutes

Purpose: Transform suffering into gateway to open-hearted awareness

Instructions:

Opening dedication and concentration

- Settle yourself in your body
- Set the intention to cultivate the qualities of your heart with this practice
- Dedicate your practice to the well-being of yourself, your loved ones, and the world
- Invoke a sense of your Field of Care
- Gather your mind by focusing on body and breath
    - Notice everything about the rising breath
    - Notice everything about the falling breath
- Pay particular attention to the exhale
    - Relax and let go with the falling breath
    - Continue letting go even beyond the end of the falling breath
    - Allow the next breath to flow in effortlessly, all by itself

- Feel breath breathing you
    - Allow your awareness to be carried on the effortless flow of breathing

Emptiness of body

- Summon your usual sense of self and personal identity
    - Gain a general awareness of your "you-ness"
    - Observe how this feels in your body
- Enhance your high-speed awareness to explore your body
    - Begin at your head, using heightened awareness to scan downward
    - Search through your jaw and neck
    - Ask: "Can I find anything solid about my sense of self here?"
- Notice how the more you search, the more your sense of self recedes as unfindable
- Continue searching through your trunk
    - Explore your chest, belly, back, shoulders, arms, and hands
    - Search for anything solid or independently existing
- Complete your search through the lower half of your body
    - Scan through pelvis, thighs, shins, feet, and toes
    - Notice how your sense of self remains unfindable
- Recognize the shift from functioning as "self" to functioning as awareness
    - Affirm what remains: awareness itself is doing the meditation
- Make one final search through your whole body
    - When you see clearly that a solid self is unfindable, affirm what remains: the field of awareness
    - Notice that your sense of self is still there, but in the background—now an event in the field of awareness, not where you're coming from

Emptiness of pain

- Focus your awareness on your chest, specifically in the area of your heart
- Notice your heart's sense
    - How are you feeling in your heart right now?
    - How is your body holding this feeling?
- Notice whatever pain is present in your heart
    - Allow yourself to truly feel this
    - Experience what you're feeling without resistance
- Let this be just as it is, and turn to recognize awareness itself
- Resting in awareness, as awareness:
    - Use your heightened awareness to explore the pain in your heart
    - Search through the pain with your attention
    - Feel: "Can I find anything solid, substantial, or independent in this pain?"
- Notice how the more you search, the more the pain recedes as unfindable
- Notice what remains after the solid pain dissolves:
    - There may still be an emotional imprint or feeling resonance
    - If there was tightness or constriction, what remains?
    - If there was frustration, what remains?
    - If there was sadness, what remains?
    - If there was heaviness of heart, what remains?
    - If there was anxiety, what remains?
    - If there was shame, what remains?
- Recognize what persists after searching:
    - A field of awareness with an emotional imprint
    - Energy that is insubstantial, changing, and flowing
    - Energy as a feeling of lightness and warmth
    - There may still be heartache, but now there's also awakeness, aliveness, meaning, and perhaps a longing for connection and love

Open-hearted awareness

- Become aware of your body as a whole
    - Observe the gentle rise and fall of your breath
    - Feel breath breathing you; breath as awareness, awareness as breath
- Notice how vast space and awareness are not separate
    - All sights and sounds are part of this non-dual field
    - No inside, no outside
- See how everything appears insubstantial yet lively
    - A vast, boundless, non-dual awareness, an ocean-like ground of being
    - Moment by moment, everything is fresh, unencumbered
    - All is arising as dancing awake awareness
    - No past, no future—everything appears lucid and new
- Experience yourself as one with this vast ocean of Loving Awareness
    - Arising as energy and form
- From this field of awareness:
    - Look back at the faint imprint, the emotional resonance that was the pain
    - Hold this suffering gently, as you would hold a newborn baby
    - Hold it with warmth and care
    - See it from the perspective of vast, ocean-like awareness
- Within this Field of Care:
    - Extend kindness and well-wishing toward yourself
    - Extend tenderness and gentleness toward others who are suffering
    - Let this care extend in ever-widening circles to our suffering world

Reflection: Feel this practice in your body, heart, and mind.

As Loch Kelly beautifully puts it: "Our pain is now infused with unconditional love. Not 'our' love, but love that just 'is.' Duality ceases to exist; ocean and waves are one, and there is just one vast, warm space: the heart of the world and awareness." That is exactly what John Makransky calls the Field of Care.

Daily Life Integration

The real test of these practices comes in daily life. Here are ways to integrate them:

Micro-Practices (30 seconds - 2 minutes):

- When upset, pause and take three conscious breaths
- Sense, "What am I feeling in my body right now?"
- Give the feeling space rather than trying to fix it immediately
- Remember that this feeling is temporary; the awareness holding it is spacious

Transition Practices:

- Before entering stressful situations, briefly connect with your Field of Care
- Use difficult emotions as reminders to practice rather than problems to solve
- When triggered, feel deeply: "How can this serve my awakening?"

End-of-Day Integration:

- Review challenging moments with compassion rather than judgment
- Reflect: "What did my pain teach me today?"
- Appreciate moments when you remembered to respond rather than react

Contemporary Relevance

Meeting Modern Challenges

Again, in our current world, these practices are not luxury items for spiritual seekers—they're essential tools for anyone navigating:

- Climate anxiety and environmental grief
- Political polarization and social division
- Survival fear concerning living expenses and jobs
- Stress around family and relationships, often increased by societal upheaval
- Health concerns, including health care and aging
- Fear of war, of growing authoritarianism, sadness for friends and neighbors who feel unsafe
- The rapidly increasing amount of real fear and danger makes many long for safety and home. Being rooted in a spiritual home provides the resilience to stay engaged and courageous on behalf of ourselves and others

Each of these current stressors can become a doorway to deeper wisdom and compassion when met with the practices outlined in this chapter.

The Ripple Effect, Which Is Important

When we learn to handle our own pain skillfully, something remarkable happens: we naturally become better at being present with others' suffering. This isn't just personal healing—it's about developing the capacity our world desperately needs.

Healthcare workers learn to stay present with patients' pain without taking it on as their own. Parents discover they can remain steady when children are struggling. Teachers find they can support students through difficult emotions. Community leaders develop the resilience needed for long-term social change work.

As Mark discovered, our own suffering becomes not just something to endure or overcome, but a source of wisdom and connection that allows us to serve others more effectively—turning even spiritual homesickness into a path of service.

Key Insights

- **Pain as teacher:** Our most difficult emotions can become gateways to wisdom and compassion rather than just obstacles to overcome
- **Spacious awareness:** We are not our pain; we are the awareness that can hold pain with love
- **Integration matters:** Spiritual practice works best when combined with psychological understanding
- **Sustainable compassion:** When care flows from awareness itself rather than personal effort, we don't burn out
- **Service emerges naturally:** As we heal our own relationship with suffering, we naturally become more available to help others. We become the "Wounded Healer."
- **Existential lostness and Spiritual homesickness as gateway:** Especially our most desperate longing for meaning and connection can become our doorway to recognizing our true nature

"It is the Pain that breaks the shell that encloses our understanding, so that its heart can stand in the sun"
-Kahlil Gibran

The pathway through pain to awakening isn't about becoming invulnerable or transcending human emotions. It's about discovering that our full humanity—including our capacity to hurt and to long for something more—can become a source of wisdom, connection, and service when held within the field of Loving Awareness that is our deepest nature.

This transformation doesn't happen overnight, but with patience, practice, and gentle persistence, even our deepest wounds and our profound spiritual homesickness can become doorways to the very qualities our world most needs: wisdom, compassion, and the courage to remain open-hearted in the face of life's challenges and dangers.

CHAPTER 10

Sustainable Compassion—Love Without Burnout

Learning to be compassionately present with our own pain, as Mark discovered, naturally opens our capacity to be present with others' suffering without burning out. But this requires more than just individual practice; it calls for what John Makransky terms 'Sustainable Compassion,' a systematic approach that draws from the inexhaustible wellspring of awareness itself—particularly crucial for healing the collective spiritual homesickness of our time.

This practice heals spiritual homesickness by teaching us to serve from the inexhaustible source instead of trying to fix what is painful with personal willpower. When we understand our fundamental interconnectedness, we see that meaningful service flows naturally from Loving Awareness.

The evening at the community center was winding down as I packed up my meditation cushions. Miguel approached me, his usually vibrant demeanor subdued. A thirty-five-year-old high school counselor who had been attending my meditation classes for about six months, Miguel had recently begun working with LGBTQ+ teens in a new school district.

"Can I talk to you for a minute?" he asked, helping me stack the remaining cushions.

We sat in the now-empty room, as late autumn sunlight cast long shadows across the wooden floor. Miguel took a deep breath; his eyes fixed on his interlaced fingers.

"Today was rough," he began. "A parent called the principal, demanding I be fired because I have a photo of my husband and me on my desk. The principal defended me, but..." His voice trailed off. "I've spent years building confidence in who I am, but this knocked me sideways. All those old feelings of shame and anger came flooding back."

Miguel's experience reflected not only personal trauma but also the broader spiritual homesickness affecting marginalized communities—the strong feeling of not belonging in a world that often rejects their authentic selves. His struggle to stay compassionate despite hatred highlighted the challenge many encounter in our divided society. This challenge can also lead many to feel disconnected from religious and spiritual communities—and even the sacred.

I nodded, listening closely.

"The worst part was feeling as if I couldn't be fully present for the students who needed me today. I was so preoccupied with my own reaction—the tightness in my chest and the racing thoughts—that I couldn't give them what they needed."

"That sounds incredibly difficult," I said. "What did you do with those feelings?"

Miguel's expression softened slightly. "That's why I wanted to talk to you. I remembered the compassionate presence practice we've been doing. During my lunch break, I found a quiet corner in my office and just sat with those feelings—the anger, the shame, the fear. I didn't try to push them away or get lost in planning what to say to the principal or the parent."

He paused and looked up. "I just let the feelings be there and gave them space. I noticed the tension in my shoulders and the heat in my face. At first, it was uncomfortable, but I stayed with it, remembering what you said about feelings needing space to find their place."

"And what happened?" I asked.

"Something shifted," Miguel said, his voice now stronger. "The feelings didn't go away, but they... opened up somehow. Beneath the anger, I found this deep concern for those kids who might be watching how this situation played out. And under the shame was this profound tenderness for the part of me that still carries old wounds."

Miguel continued, "By the afternoon, I felt clearer, more spacious inside. A student came in—a girl who's been struggling with her own identity—and for the first time, I could truly be there for her without my own story getting in the way. I wasn't caught up in my reactions anymore. I could see her more clearly."

I recognized in Miguel's experience something I had seen many times—how practicing compassionate presence to feelings not only fosters inner healing but also builds a deeper ability to be fully present with others.

"You know," Miguel said, "before I started these practices, I would have either suppressed those feelings or been totally consumed by them. Either way, I wouldn't have been available to that student in the way she needed me to be."

"It's remarkable how being compassionately present to our own feelings changes the way we can connect with others," I reflected.

Miguel nodded. "It feels like the more I practice this way of being with my feelings, the more I can be a steady presence for these kids who are facing their own battles. And maybe that's the most powerful thing I can offer them—not answers or advice, but this way of being present to whatever arises, without turning away."

As Miguel gathered his belongings to leave, I noticed a new steadiness in him, a quiet confidence that came not from avoiding difficulty but from learning to face it in a healing way.

His story embodies the sustainable compassion practices I've shared in this book. They're not just techniques for personal well-being, but a way to be more present and responsive to suffering in our world without burning out, while offering healing medicine for the epidemic of spiritual homesickness that affects so many.

As we heal our own spiritual homesickness through sustainable compassion practices, we naturally become a source of healing for others experiencing the same collective disconnection. Miguel's transformation allowed him to serve marginalized students from a place of genuine presence rather than defensive reaction.

I discussed the Field of Care in Chapters 2 and 8 and its crucial role in our spiritual and psychological growth. I will now introduce you to the specific practices developed by John Makransky and how he incorporates those practices into a comprehensive care approach. This creates a powerful system for supporting sustainable care for yourself and others.

Sustainable Compassion Training (SCT)

My mentor John Makransky, a wonderful contemplative teacher, developed a series of practices that capture this fundamental insight.

He calls it "Sustainable Compassion," the direct experience of compassion arising naturally from our deepest ground of being into accessible practices for everyday life.

What I love about John's approach is how it respects both ancient wisdom traditions and modern psychological insights. His sustainable compassion practices build a bridge between the deep non-dual awareness practices we've been exploring and the everyday challenge of maintaining compassion in a troubled world—especially important for healing spiritual homesickness, which is fundamentally about disconnection from love and meaning.

The Receptive Mode: Learning to Receive Care

What makes John's approach unique is that it doesn't start with self-care or caring for others, but with receiving care—the love and warmth that are naturally part of the ground of being itself. We don't need to create this essential warmth from scratch; it is already present within the nature of awareness, along with knowing, stillness, and clarity. This is similar to what we see in attachment theory—the safety and love we get from caregivers help us build our own ability to care for others.

We may realize that we need to learn how to receive and accept love. Many of us weren't taught to do that and feel safer not expecting anything from others, or we feel more comfortable and in control when giving to others. However, it's a wonderful experience to learn how to receive—to let ourselves be vulnerable and open to kindness and generosity from others and from life. Then, we can give freely without burning out.

This is especially important for those experiencing spiritual homesickness, who often feel isolated from sources of love and support. Learning to accept care helps heal the deep sense of not belonging that characterizes this ailment.

In the receptive mode of SCT, we purposefully reconnect with moments when we felt truly seen, accepted, or loved. We recall the caregivers, benefactors, mentors, or spiritual figures who made us feel cared for. When we fully embody these experiences, we activate the caring qualities that already exist within the foundation of awareness, even if they are temporarily hidden by stress, doubt, or fear.

This isn't just wishful thinking or visualization. When we recall such moments, they become fully embodied experiences, filled with all the qualities of care, love, warmth, acceptance, and well-being that once accompanied them. *(On a Personal Note: see below)*[33]

A Universal Approach

What I find especially beautiful about this approach is its inclusivity. Some people connect with spiritual figures from their traditions, others with personal memories of being cared for, and still others with moments in nature when they felt a deep sense of peace. John calls this an "open secular space" that welcomes people of diverse worldviews; I might call this space "secular and sacred."

---

[33] ***On a Personal Note:*** *My gradual road to deeply understand compassion practices, which started with Sharon Salzberg's Loving Kindness as wholesome intention, dropped deeper as I discovered warmth and care as qualities of the deepest ground of being. Then, with John Makransky, my compassion practice received another nudge towards depth. When John talks about sustainable compassion, he differentiates the receptive mode, the deepening mode, and the inclusive mode. I had to work for a while with these practices to deeply understand his point.*

When hearing about the receptive mode, I realized that it was not easy for me to allow myself to "receive" something that is good. I am a better giver than receiver. Receiving the goodness and blessing of the Field of Care, now primed by figures of those who supported and loved me, was at first not easy.

The easiest figure to inspire my Field of Care has been Joanna Macy with her unbridled love, joy, warmth, and helpfulness.

I can see myself sitting always at the same place on her couch, with her listening carefully to me, answering thoughtfully and brilliantly, while beaming with joy. I feel that moment of loving attention as warmth and energy in my body and heart. I am grateful for that gift.

Only when my receptive mode is well-established and sturdy can I now welcome difficult feelings, like sadness or fear.

I've seen this approach work remarkably well in my own teaching. David, an atheist scientist, connects with the memory of his grandfather's unconditional acceptance. Fatima, a devout Muslim, feels embraced by Allah's compassion. Sarah, who follows no particular spiritual path, recalls the deep peace she felt while watching a sunset over the ocean. Each person accesses the same Field of Care through their own genuine doorway—healing their specific form of spiritual homesickness.

The second receptive mode practice involves becoming more deeply open to love and compassion by recognizing and accepting the challenging parts of ourselves. When challenges arise during meditation—such as feeling unworthy of care or resisting receiving love—we are encouraged to notice these parts and allow them to be embraced within the Field of Care.

This shows a deep understanding: true healing doesn't come from avoiding the tough parts of our experience but from allowing them to be present in a space of compassionate awareness, just as Miguel experienced in his story.

Practice: Welcoming Difficult Parts

Time Needed: 10-15 minutes

Purpose: Include challenging aspects of yourself in the Field of Care— this practice offers healing for personal hurts, societal anguish, as well as addressing a painful existential crisis and doubt by creating a loving space for all aspects of our experience

Instructions:

- Begin by connecting with the Field of Care using the previous practice
- Once you feel that connection, notice if there's any resistance to receiving care
- There might be a voice saying "I don't deserve this" or a feeling of unworthiness or shame
- Notice if spiritual homesickness arises—that sense of not belonging or being fundamentally flawed

- Instead of pushing this difficulty away, turn toward it with gentle curiosity
- Ask yourself: Where do I feel this in my body? What is its texture, shape, or color?
- Without trying to change it, simply acknowledge: "This too is part of my experience right now"
- Imagine the Field of Care expanding to include this challenging aspect
- Like a loving parent embracing a struggling child, let this resistance or unworthiness be held in awareness
- Observe what happens when you allow both the care and the difficulty to coexist

Reflection: Feel this practice in your body, heart, and mind.

The Deepening Mode: Compassionate Presence to Feelings

In deepening practice, we access the caring qualities within our awareness by cultivating compassionate presence toward our feelings. Instead of suppressing difficult emotions or acting them out, we learn to welcome them into a compassionate space where they can settle naturally.

The practice involves four simple steps:

1. Notice the feelings within any state of mind or body that's occurring.
2. Allow the feeling to take all the space it needs to find its own place.
3. Rest with or within the feeling.
4. Then simply allow everything to exist with spaciousness.

When we establish this holding environment where emotions aren't elaborated on or reacted to, something remarkable happens—

the process of constructing an emotion can relax and unwind, revealing its empty nature.

I've seen this practice transform people's relationships with difficult emotions—including the complex feelings associated with spiritual homesickness. Thomas, a combat veteran with PTSD, described how it changed his experience of anger: "Before, when anger came, I'd either explode or shut down completely. Now I can feel the heat and energy of it in my body without being overwhelmed by it. There's this space around it that wasn't there before. The anger still comes, but it doesn't define me anymore."

Practice: Compassionate Presence to Difficult Emotions

Time Needed: 5-20 minutes (as needed)

Purpose: To develop a new relationship with challenging emotions— healing existential and spiritual lostness by creating a loving space for all emotional experiences

Instructions:

- When you notice a challenging emotion arising—anxiety, anger, sadness, or the deep longing of spiritual homesickness—pause
- Acknowledge the feeling: "I'm feeling anxious right now" or "There's anger here," or "I notice my spiritual homesickness"
- Notice where and how this emotion manifests in your body
    - Is there tightness in your chest?
    - A knot in your stomach?
    - Heat in your face?
- Instead of attempting to change this feeling or making up a story about why it's happening, give it space to be fully felt
- Imagine your awareness as a spacious room that can easily accommodate this emotion

- Rest in the feeling, breathing with it, allowing it to be exactly as it is
- You might place a hand gently on the area where you feel the emotion most strongly
- Notice that there is both the feeling itself and the awareness that recognizes the feeling—the awareness that recognizes your pain with warmth is the Field of Care
- Allow both to coexist without preference or resistance
- Observe how the emotion may begin to shift and change naturally, not because you're trying to make it go away, but because you're allowing it to unfold organically

Reflection: Feel this practice in your body, heart, and mind.

(On a Personal Note: see below)[34]

---

[34] ***On a Personal Note:*** *"Compassionate Presence to Difficult Emotions" meant going again a step deeper with my compassion practice. Much of my spiritual life has included detaching from difficult emotions. With mindfulness meditation, we learned naming difficult emotions and letting them pass through—maybe first naming and feeling them, but then letting them pass through. There was still an element of detachment.*

In Mahamudra meditations there was again a preference for detachment. The more we recede into the field of Awake Awareness (as Mahamudra calls it), the further away are we from the nitty gritty. Only, when we hover in a completely open space, a space beyond the separate self, then a kind of universal compassion comes up.

John Makransky's approach asks us to fully invite the uncomfortable. Yes, we have the back of the Field of Care, but the pain is still pain. It is held as long as it needs to be there within the Field of Care, with all its hurt and discomfort. This demands of me full acceptance, to be with myself like a mother would be with a crying, sick child. And there is something so healing and strengthening in this paradoxical move. I learned here a deep readiness and willingness to be with whatever there is.

As I allow this process of acceptance of what is difficult to happen, there is a deepening. Eventually, the core of the hurt transforms into peace.

"Letting Be" in Body, Breath, and Mind

Here's a revised version of the Letting Be practice from Chapter 6, "Tasting the Field." The deepening mode allows us to experience the deepest level through "letting be" in body, breath, and mind. This practice helps us settle into the pervasive openness, simplicity, and clarity of our fundamental awareness. The deeper our roots grow, the more we can welcome and include what is difficult. The more we can be generous, kind, and forgiving toward what arises from the hidden crevices of our own psyche or toward what comes toward us from the world around us—including the complex feelings linked to isolation, lack of belonging, deeply held anger, as well as spiritual homesickness. *(On a Personal Note: see below)*[35]

Practice: Letting Be

Time Needed: 10-20 minutes

Purpose: To settle into the pervasive openness of fundamental awareness—healing isolation, rejection, frustration, as well as existential doubt and weariness by recognizing our natural state of being—our home.

Instructions:

1. Sit comfortably with your eyes slightly open, gazing softly downward
2. Begin with your body
    - Simply notice your body as it is right now
    - Feel the weight of your body supported by your seat
    - Notice any areas of tension or ease

[35] ***On a Personal Note:*** *Each time I practice the "Letting Be" meditation, I feel the roots of my metaphorical spirit-tree grow a little deeper, and become a little stronger. Especially when my feelings of spiritual homesickness, my longing for home is especially strong, the "Letting Be" practice gives me a place to just be, to heal, and to slowly grow.*

    - Instead of trying to relax actively, simply allow your body to be as it is
    - There's nothing to fix or improve—just this body, as it is, in this moment
    - Let the body sense of feeling draw you into its depth
3. Move to your breath
    - Observe the natural rhythm of your breath without controlling it
    - Your body breathes on its own—you don't need to consciously breathe
    - Just as waves rise and fall in the ocean, your breath rises and falls
    - Let breath draw you into its depth
4. Include your mind
    - Pay attention to your mind and its activity
    - Thoughts, emotions, and sensations arise and fade away
    - Instead of getting caught up in them or pushing them away, simply allow them to exist
    - If lostness and existential angst arise—that deep longing or sense of not belonging—welcome it with the same open allowing
    - Recognize the spacious awareness that is aware of all these experiences
    - Let awareness draw you into its depths
5. Rest in this awareness that already knows and holds everything
    - Let the ground of being draw you into its depth
6. When you notice you've become caught in thought, gently return to this simple letting be of body, breath, and mind together
    - Let the ground of being as awareness and space draw you into its depth
    - And let everything be

Reflection: Feel this practice in your body, heart, and mind.

The Inclusive Mode: Extending Care to Others

The inclusive mode allows us to extend care and compassion to others in a way that feels unconditional, inclusive, and sustainable. What makes this approach uniquely sustainable is that we don't try to generate compassion from nothing. Instead, we let the caring energy we've accessed in the receptive mode flow through us to others. We learn to hold others as we are held, and to see them as we are seen.

In this mode, we go beyond the narrow and fixed impressions we form of others, connecting with their deeper dignity and potential. We understand that beneath everyone's surface behavior, no matter how difficult it might be, there remains the same capacity for awareness, clarity, and care that we've found in ourselves.

Practice: Extending Care

Time Needed: 5-10 minutes

Purpose: Build genuine connections beyond surface impressions—healing loneliness, rejection, frustration, and also spiritual lostness by recognizing our shared humanity

Instructions:

1. Take a comfortable seated position and settle your awareness
2. Consider someone you meet regularly—a colleague, neighbor, or family member
3. Notice the impressions or judgments you usually form about this person
4. Now, imagine this person beyond these surface impressions
    - Consider that they, like you, have hopes, fears, and dreams
    - They, too, have experienced joy and sorrow, success and disappointment

- They may be carrying their own form of spiritual homesickness—their own deep longing for meaning and belonging
- Beneath their visible behaviors lie invisible longings—for connection, understanding, and peace

5. As you hold this person in mind, allow the Field of Care you've been cultivating to extend to them
6. You are becoming a healing environment for their being
7. You're not forcing yourself to feel anything in particular—simply let them be embraced by the same spacious awareness that holds you
8. Notice if there's a shift in how you perceive this person
9. Perhaps you sense a deeper connection or feel more open to them as they are, rather than how you wish they would be
10. Imagine those who are suffering from spiritual homesickness, now being held and healed by the Field of Care

Reflection: Feel this practice in your body, heart, and mind.

Generating Compassion Through Our Suffering

One of the most powerful aspects of SCT is its ability to change how we relate to suffering, especially the sorrow of separation, which leads to so much isolation, feeling hurt and unsafe, and even spiritual homesickness. *(On a Personal Note: see below)*[36] Instead

---

[36] ***On a Personal Note:*** *Long before I met John Makransky, I had reflected on something like an inclusive mode. As the granddaughter of a historian who was incarcerated by the Nazis in WWII Germany, I have been pondering how to help those who suffer in the world. As a post-war German, I wanted to help all others who suffer from racism, poverty, and discrimination. My mother carried the torch forward when she was the only doctor who treated Turkish guestworkers and other immigrants in town. I travelled with her from house to house. I saw her burn out and get very sick and tired.*

When I was working in hospitals and then with trauma as a psychologist, I witnessed my colleagues burn out and shut down right and left.

I felt protected by my spiritual practice, which I had all along.

of viewing pain as something to escape or move past, we learn to use it as a path to greater compassion for ourselves and others. We are learning to become a healing space for our own painful feelings.

In a remarkable practice, we intentionally allow ourselves to experience difficult emotions, supported by our secure inner foundation of Loving Awareness. As we feel these emotions, we realize that many others go through similar feelings in their own ways. Suddenly, our suffering isn't isolating but connecting—it's a bridge instead of a barrier.

This is especially powerful in the context of a lack of belonging and spiritual homesickness. When we realize that millions of people share this deep longing for meaning and connection, our individual sense of disconnection and alienation transforms into compassionate understanding of our shared human experience.

Practice: From Personal Pain to Universal Compassion

Time Needed: 10-15 minutes

Purpose: To turn personal suffering into compassionate connection—healing isolation, and spiritual homesickness by recognizing our shared human experience

---

Joanna taught me about the "Great Immensity," the Field of Loving Awareness, that allows our hearts to break in the face of suffering-with love.

John Makransky gave me a complementary practice, a practice that is methodical, step by step. Joanna and John allow me to follow my inclination toward social engagement, of including the poor, the ones in danger, the so-called outsiders. Now I gain energy rather than get depleted.

This is a difficult time in our country. Many around me shut down. I can't. I am grateful to have found a practice that helps me to gain energy through social engagement, rather than burn out. For me, passivity is followed by depression. Now, when I start to feel depressed, I become creative. What new essay could I write to wake people up, what new group would be helpful as a safe place in our town? Let's be creative together!

Instructions:

1. Begin by connecting with the Field of Care, feeling supported and held in awareness
2. From this secure base, softly recall a challenging situation or feeling you're presently facing
   - It could be anxiety about the future
   - Grief over a loss
   - Concern about the state of our world
   - The deep longing following existential lostness
3. As you experience this difficulty, acknowledge it fully: "This is hard. This hurts."
4. Rest your hand on your heart if that feels comforting.
5. Now, expand your view to see that many others are experiencing this kind of suffering right now
   - Perhaps millions of people are experiencing anxiety, grief, or concern similar to yours
   - Countless others share this same lack of belonging as well as an existential and spiritual lack of home—this longing for deeper meaning, authentic connection, safety, and freedom
   - This acknowledgment helps place your suffering within a larger human context
6. Silently acknowledge: "Just as I'm experiencing this difficulty, so are many others. May we all find ease. May we all be held in care"
7. Notice how this shift in perspective affects your relationship with your own suffering
8. Many people find that their pain becomes both more manageable and more meaningful when seen within this larger context of shared humanity
9. Imagine those who are troubled being held and healed by the Field of Care now

Reflection: Feel this practice in your body, heart, and mind.

Generating a Strong Will for Compassionate Action

Another aspect of SCT helps us build strong motivation and the ability for compassionate action in the world. When we see others' suffering, we intentionally allow our empathy to transform into a powerful energy of compassion. Instead of retreating inward and getting stuck in empathic or moral distress, we direct our empathetic focus outward toward those in need.

A key insight here is that we are protected from burnout by understanding that suffering is never the only truth—it is always part of a larger context of openness, warmth, and care, where transformation and healing can happen. This is especially important when addressing the collective existential crisis or poverty and spiritual homesickness of our time—we can respond to widespread disconnection and meaninglessness without succumbing to despair.

Practice: From Empathy to Compassionate Action

Time Needed: 5-15 minutes

Purpose: To transform empathy into sustainable, compassionate action—healing our lack of belonging by channeling our care into effective service

Instructions:

1. When you encounter someone's suffering, whether directly in your life or through news about the world, pause
2. First, acknowledge the natural empathetic response: "This is painful to witness"
3. Notice if there's a tendency to either
   - Shut down (turning away from the suffering)
   - Become overwhelmed (taking the suffering into yourself without any boundary)
4. Instead, ground yourself in the field of awareness and care

5. Feel supported and held in this awareness
6. From this grounded place, turn toward the suffering you're witnessing with a conscious intention: "May my empathy become energy for action rather than distress"
7. Imagine your care flowing outward as a tangible force, not from personal depletion but from the inexhaustible field of awareness itself
8. You might be helpful through practical action, offering your presence, or simply holding those who suffer in your heart with genuine care
9. If you're witnessing collective danger, exclusion of minorities—people struggling with violence, meaninglessness, disconnection, or despair—imagine them being held and healed by the Field of Care
10. Imagine them being happy, loved, and living in a more compassionate world where authentic connection and meaning are available to all.

Reflection: Feel this practice in your body, heart, and mind.

Sustainable Engagement in a Troubled World

As we face the huge challenges of our troubled world—wars internationally, violence and societal disarray domestically, spiritual uprootedness—these practices provide a way to stay engaged without burning out. They help turn our empathy for suffering from a source of distress into a source of lasting, brave action.

What Miguel found in working with vulnerable students reflects the core of these practices: by learning to be compassionately aware of our own feelings, we improve our ability to be fully present for others without being overwhelmed by their pain or our reactions. We become able to respond with wisdom and love instead of fear or avoidance.

I've seen this change in my student Elena, the environmental activist who was close to burnout. "Before learning these practices," she told me, "Every new report on climate change would send me into either panic or despair. I was either frantically active or completely paralyzed. Now I can stay present with the reality of our situation without being overwhelmed by it. I still feel the urgency, but it comes with a strange kind of peace too—like I'm being held by something much larger than myself as I do this work."

As we grow our own spiritual roots and gain a deep resilience through sustainable compassion practices, we naturally become a source of healing for others experiencing the same collective disconnection. Elena's transformation allowed her to serve the environmental movement from a place of love instead of desperate fear.

Embracing Our Full Humanity

These practices don't ask us to go beyond our humanity but to fully embrace it, recognizing that our vulnerability and suffering can bond us more deeply with others instead of dividing us. They provide a way to expand our circle of concern while staying connected to the endless well of care at the heart of our awareness.

In a world that often feels more fragmented and divided—where spiritual uprootedness, lack of belonging and existential homesickness has become widespread—sustainable compassion reminds us that beneath our differences, there is a common basis of awareness and caring. As we learn to access this foundation more regularly, we discover resources for compassion and connection that we didn't realize we had.

The path isn't straight but spirals—we'll keep returning to the receptive mode, strengthening our connection to the Field of Care and then reaching outward with renewed compassion. This mirrors life itself, with its rhythm of turning inward and reaching outward, receiving and giving.

As you do these exercises, be gentle with yourself. Some days, they will come easily and feel natural; other days, they might seem hard or far away. What matters is your ongoing effort to connect with the sense of care that is already around you, letting it nourish and support you as you move through our beautiful but troubled world.

May these practices serve as faithful companions on your journey, helping you discover the profound truth that Miguel, Elena, and many others have found: when compassion flows from an awakened heart, there are no limits to how deeply we can care without becoming exhausted. Your open heart becomes not a burden but a gift to yourself and a blessing to our world in need, offering healing medicine for the epidemic of social and existential uprootedness, as well as spiritual homesickness affecting so many.

Bringing These Practices Into Socially Engaged Spirituality

For those of you walking the dual path of deep spiritual practice and social engagement, these methods create an essential link between inner transformation and outer service. When you volunteer at community centers, participate in climate initiatives, advocate for fair healthcare, work to heal political divisions, engage in political protest, write an essay supporting the rule of law, or simply aim to be a force for good in helping others to feel a sense of belonging and safety, you connect your inner growth with real actions that make a difference.

The receptive mode becomes your sanctuary when you feel overwhelmed by the magnitude of suffering you witness; rather than engaging in spiritual bypassing, it grounds you in a Field of Care substantial enough to embrace both your heartache for the world and your commitment to serve it. Before entering difficult conversations about social issues or community needs, taking even two minutes to practice "letting be" can shift your entire presence from reactive to responsive.

When faced with setbacks—failed projects, resistance to change, or daunting systemic issues—the compassionate presence of feelings practice lets you honor your disappointment and frustration without being defined by them. This inclusive approach changes how you see those with different perspectives, helping you recognize their inherent dignity while clearly expressing your values.

As socially engaged spiritual practitioners have always understood, true compassion involves both inner reflection and outward action. These practices foster this integration by connecting your spiritual depth with your social awareness, allowing each to support and enhance the other rather than compete for your limited energy.

Within this harmony lies the secret to sustainable engagement—you no longer need to choose between inner peace and social responsibility, or between Loving Awareness and ethical action. Instead, like water flowing from an endless spring, your social engagement naturally reflects your spiritual realization, and your spiritual practice becomes more genuine through its connection with real-world issues.

The sustainable compassion practices help ensure that your service comes from an inexhaustible wellspring rather than personal willpower. This is particularly important when working to heal the collective existential lostness and spiritual homesickness of our time—a task that requires sustained compassion and wisdom over many years.

This is the awakened engagement our interconnected world urgently needs—people whose hearts stay both tender and strong, who can face difficult truths without losing hope, and who draw from a never-ending well of compassion.

When we serve from the Field of Care itself, we discover that helping others heal their spiritual homesickness simultaneously deepens our own connection to meaning and purpose. We become part of the solution to our world's deepest needs while finding our own deepest fulfillment—not through personal achievement, but through recognizing our essential role in the healing of our existentially lost and spiritually homesick world.

CHAPTER 11

Engaged Awareness—When Practice Becomes Service

Sustainable compassion practices give us tools to stay open-hearted in a tough world, but how do we make this way of being part of our daily lives? We need practical ways to weave Loving Awareness into our work, relationships, and daily duties—offering healing presence to a world suffering from spiritual homesickness. The journey of engaged awareness starts with incorporating practice into life, moment by moment.

This practice offers healing for existential lostness, societal fear and spiritual homesickness by transforming daily life into meaningful service. When we learn to live from Loving Awareness throughout our activities, ordinary work becomes sacred service, relationships become opportunities for mutual healing, and every interaction becomes a chance to offer medicine to our spiritually homesick world.

Dr. Michael's Story: Healing Presence in Action

"Every day, as I walk from home to the hospital, I feel the contact between the soles of my feet and the Earth, which becomes a gateway to deeper awareness. My heart opens to a sense of spaciousness, an ease of being that feels both wide awake and grounded."

Dr. Michael Kearney, a palliative care physician in his early seventies with decades of experience, explains how he incorporates Loving Awareness practice into his work with seriously ill and dying patients. What drew him to this specialty was hearing someone describe St. Christopher's Hospice in London, the first modern hospice where he trained, as "a place of healing."

"My years in medicine have been a journey to understand what healing truly means and what it means to be a healer," he explains. "Healing, in the sense of becoming whole, is possible even when a cure is no longer possible,"

Dr. Michael sees his work as addressing not only physical pain but also the spiritual longing that often grows stronger when people confront their mortality—the deep questions about meaning, purpose, and what truly matters that come to the surface when life is limited.

Beyond Medical Interventions

Throughout his career, Dr. Michael sought ways to help patients beyond just medical treatments and medications. "For years, I was on a journey of psychological understanding, fascinated by the idea of the wounded healer," he shares. "The wounded healer describes a person whose own healing journey and wounds have led them to become a healer to others. Being present as a wounded healer helps to awaken a patient's innate healing capacity."

He has come to realize that healing depends more on who caregivers are as individuals than on their skills and interventions. "I've realized the truth in the phrase 'we are the medicine,'" he says. "My spiritual journey isn't just about the benefits I receive but about the quality of presence I bring to each encounter, to every patient."

In recent years, Dr. Michael has become interested in contemplative psychology and practice, finding that awareness teachings resonate well with other wisdom traditions he has studied, such as Earth-based spirituality and Native American teachings.

Practical Integration in Healthcare

Loving Awareness practices have helped Michael stay present even during challenging encounters. "I've come to trust that the patient and I are already held in a field of awareness, and that it's my quality of presence that helps to awaken the patient to this. When I'm resting in this deeper ground, others can intuitively feel it, and their hearts open to it." He believes that his presence at the bedside is his most valuable contribution.

"I listen carefully to how a person is doing and ask about their pain. And, of course, I use the skills I've gained over the years to intervene and do what I can to help, but ultimately, I trust in the quality of presence."

Dr. Michael has developed practical strategies for maintaining Loving Awareness throughout his workday. "Every morning, as I walk to work, I practice emptiness—recognizing that my solid sense of self is actually fluid and open—and then I settle into Loving Awareness. Then, when I reach the office, open the door, and see my colleagues with questions or the sticky notes on my computer, poof... I immediately fall out of this expanded awareness. Sometimes I recognize this and set the intention to re-establish it."

Creating Daily Reminders

He has developed prompts to help himself reconnect throughout the day. "I've learned to pay attention to the sensation of contact between my feet and the ground. When I become aware of this feeling, I think to myself, 'the pads of my feet are touching the ground that connects me to something larger.' Sometimes, this brings me back into Loving Awareness.

"I do these brief awareness practices throughout the day," he continues. "Sometimes my inner observer notices that I'm wrapped up in conceptual thinking or caught in emotional reactions. And then there are other times when Loving Awareness emerges spontaneously."

He has noticed that certain situations naturally evoke Loving Awareness. "Sometimes, when I find myself in a place of deep listening, when people are truly open in their hearts or when I'm in the presence of someone close to death, Loving Awareness is effortlessly there. It seems that approaching death burns away much of what is superficial, insincere, and irrelevant. What's left is the person in their essence. They become transparent, and awareness becomes palpable. As they settle into this deeper presence, it opens for me as well. The proximity of death lifts the veil between ordinary and sacred awareness."

The Journey Home

Dr. Michael has also incorporated practice into his journey home from work. "On my walk home, I do a resting in awareness practice. As my personal sense of self recedes into the background, I become more spacious. I walk home through a forested area and often feel welcomed by the trees, which I experience as expressions of this living awareness. I feel such relief in their presence at the end of a hard day. They help me release the accumulated stress."

Dr. Michael shared a recent example: "Last week, I worked with a patient experiencing significant pain—both physical and emotional, including a deep spiritual homesickness as she questioned whether her life had any meaning. Instead of immediately jumping to medical interventions, I spent the first few minutes simply resting in what I call 'Loving Awareness.' The quality of my presence changed noticeably. The patient's breathing slowed, her face softened, and she was able to share her deepest fears about dying and her sense of having lived a meaningless life. In that space of aware presence, healing happened at a level no medication could reach—a recognition that meaning wasn't something she had to achieve but something inherent in the Loving Awareness that was her deepest nature."

As we heal our own spiritual homesickness through engaged awareness, we naturally become medicine for others experiencing similar existential concerns. Dr. Michael's integration of practice and service demonstrates how professional duties can become expressions of sacred service when approached from Loving Awareness.

Weaving Loving Awareness Into Daily Life

How can we incorporate Loving Awareness into our everyday routines? We all lead different lives—some of us go to work, others work from home, some care for children, others study, some are retired, and others look after loved ones, neighbors, grandchildren, or parents. Some are physically and mentally healthy, while others face significant physical, mental, or emotional challenges.

Dr. Michael's journey through the day as a palliative care physician serves as a model for all our daily experiences. His idea of healing involves allowing ourselves to be touched by the sacred, even as we complete our everyday tasks. He demonstrates how our quality of presence—our depth of awareness—is what most helps those around us find their footing and balance again, something particularly important in a world where spiritual homesickness has reached epidemic proportions.

Adapting Practices to Your Life

We can adapt and personalize our practices to match our individual life situations. Short awareness exercises are especially useful because they are simple and quick. They can be practiced when we have only a little time, when we are on the go, using public transportation, or even in circumstances where we expect frequent interruptions.

One way to integrate brief practices into our daily lives is to use prompts to remind ourselves to practice. For example, we can do this while:

- Making a cup of coffee or tea
- Walking to our car
- Being stuck in traffic
- Waiting for a bus or riding the subway
- Standing in line at the store
- Before checking emails or social media
- When noticing the deep restlessness of spiritual homesickness arising

Creative Reminder Systems

- One practitioner programmed his computer to announce a ten-minute awareness break every hour and a half

- Another set her smartphone alarm to beep hourly as a gentle reminder
- A third person set "recognize awareness" as the password on her computer
- Some people use transition moments—doorways, elevators, red lights—as cues to pause and reconnect
- Many find it helpful to use moments of spiritual homesickness as reminders to connect with Loving Awareness

During lunch breaks, practicing mindful eating can be helpful. As Dr. Michael mentioned, he uses the times when he walks alone down hospital hallways to engage in mindful walking, letting the feel of his feet on the ground remind him to stay present.

Setting aside time in the morning for a longer practice helps start the day on a positive note. Some people prefer a special outdoor spot, while others might practice during their commute. Some listen to guided meditations while driving to work, while others do online guided meditations at home.

A Daily Rhythm of Practice

Here's a complete program for integrating Loving Awareness into your daily routine. Try this method or modify it to suit your situation. See what works best for you, and then personalize your own version.

Morning Foundation Practice

We might start the day by setting an intention to stay balanced and open-hearted, and to be a caring presence for ourselves and the others we meet. Then, we ground ourselves in the sensations of our bodies and breath through focusing practices. After a restless night's sleep, practices that address the fluid nature of our sense of self or emotions can be helpful. A practice that heightens our awareness of the field of consciousness helps build this expanded view as our foundation—especially useful for addressing any spiritual homesickness that might come up during the day.

Morning Grounding (5-10 minutes)

- Settle into your body, feeling the sensations of contact with your chair, bed, or cushion
- Notice your breath without trying to control it
- As thoughts arise, gently return to the sensation of breathing
- Feel your body as a whole, alive and present in this moment
- Set your intention: "May I remain grounded in awareness, open-hearted, and helpful to others today—offering healing presence to our spiritually homesick world."

Quick Morning Reset (2 minutes if time is short)

- Three conscious breaths, feeling your whole body
- Brief moment of gratitude for the day ahead
- Simple intention: "May I be present and kind today"

Integrating Practice Throughout the Day

Brief awareness practices can be easily incorporated into our daily routines. By consistently connecting with the field of awareness, they help us shift away from solely ego-driven perspectives and make Loving Awareness our primary way of functioning—providing natural medicine for spiritual homesickness.

Midday Micro-Practices (30 seconds to 2 minutes)

The Awareness Behind Thoughts Practice

- Notice you're having thoughts
- Ask: "Who or what is aware of these thoughts?"
- Feel the spacious Loving Awareness that notices the thoughts
- Rest in this awareness for a breath or two

This can be done while:

- Waiting for an elevator
- Standing in line
- Before responding to a phone call or email
- During commercial breaks
- While your computer loads
- When noticing spiritual homesickness arising

Traffic Light Meditation

- Use red lights as reminders to take three conscious breaths
- Feel your hands on the steering wheel, your body in the seat
- Notice the space of Loving Awareness that holds both calm and any impatience

Digital Transition Practice

Before opening your phone, computer, or any device

- Take one conscious breath
- Set an intention for how you want to engage
- Create a brief moment of Loving Awareness before entering the digital world

Lunch Break Restoration

During a lunch break, if time permits, a fifteen to twenty-minute practice can be transformative. The practice of viewing specific concerns from an expanded awareness perspective is especially helpful because it places our worries in a wider context—including concerns about meaning and purpose that characterize spiritual homesickness.

Lunch Break Integration (10-20 minutes if possible)

- Begin with 3-5 minutes of focused, yet relaxed, natural breathing to settle your mind

- Practice "Seeing Challenges from Expanded Perspective"
    - Establish the field of awareness through gentle concentration
    - From this vast perspective, look at a particular concern or challenge you're facing, including any sense of spiritual homesickness or meaninglessness
    - Notice how it appears within the field of awareness—still present, but held in a wider context
    - Feel how this shift in perspective changes your relationship to the situation
    - Return to your afternoon with this broader view

Brief Lunch Practice (5 minutes)

- Mindful eating for the first few minutes
- Pause between bites to appreciate nourishment
- Feel gratitude for the hands that grew and prepared your food
- Set intention for the afternoon

Evening Integration

We often experience periods of stress and emotional intensity during our day. We might encounter others who are struggling, read upsetting headlines, or see distressing scenes in our communities or around the world. As we get home or near the end of our workday, we often carry emotional leftovers from these experiences—including the accumulated weight of witnessing widespread spiritual homesickness in our culture.

Evening Release and Integration (15-20 minutes)

Initial Settling (5 minutes)

- Begin with slow, deep, and natural breathing
- Scan your body for areas of tension and consciously soften them

Processing the Day's Emotions

- Notice any difficult emotions that remain from your day
- Use gentle, Loving Awareness to observe these emotions in your body
- Sense their changing, impermanent nature
- Feel how they are held within the vast field of awareness
- Practice self-compassion for any challenges you faced, including moments of spiritual homesickness

Field of Care Integration

- Connect with your Field of Care using previous practices
- Once you feel that loving presence, acknowledge any painful experiences from the day
- Instead of pushing difficulties away, turn toward them with gentle curiosity
- Ask yourself: "Where do I feel this in my body? What does it need?"
- Without trying to fix anything, acknowledge: "This too is part of my human experience"
- Imagine the Field of Care expanding to embrace these challenging aspects
- Like a loving parent holding a tired child, let your day's struggles be held in awareness
- End by resting in this embodied sense of care as you prepare for sleep

Quick Evening Practice (5 minutes)

- Three minutes of grateful reflection on positive moments from the day
- Two minutes of releasing any tension or worry
- Brief intention for restful sleep and tomorrow's possibilities

Specific Applications for Different Life Situations

For Parents

- Use diaper changes, feeding times, or bedtime routines as opportunities for present-moment awareness
- When children experience strong emotions, ground yourself in awareness before responding
- Turn tantrums and meltdowns into chances to practice staying calm and present

For Healthcare Workers

- Brief awareness practice before entering each patient's room
- Use hand-washing as a mindfulness anchor—focusing on water temperature, soap texture, and the care you're giving.
- Between patients, take three mindful breaths to release the previous encounter and arrive refreshed for the next.

For Teachers

- Begin each class with a brief moment of silent presence (you don't need to call it meditation)
- Use transitions between subjects as chances for quick awareness exercises
- When students challenge you, remember they are fellow human beings deserving of compassion—possibly struggling with their own spiritual homesickness

For Office Workers

- Use bathroom breaks as chances for short walking meditation
- Practice awareness while waiting for meetings to start
- Transform commute time into practice time instead of stress time

For Caregivers of Elderly or Ill Family Members

- Remain present and mindful before difficult conversations
- Use routine care activities like assisting with meals and medications as opportunities to demonstrate loving presence
- Remember that your presence is just as healing as your practical help

For Students

- Brief Loving Awareness practices between classes or study sessions
- Use academic pressure as an opportunity to practice staying calm under stress
- Transform test anxiety by connecting with the expansive Loving Awareness that can hold all emotions

For Those Experiencing Existential Doubt and Spiritual Homesickness

- Use moments of deep longing as reminders to connect with Loving Awareness
- Practice seeing your seeking itself as arising within the awareness you're seeking
- Remember that emotional and spiritual heartache often holds wisdom—it's the soul's recognition that depth is calling you

Working with Common Challenges

"I Don't Have Time"

The beauty of engaged awareness is that it doesn't take extra time—it transforms the time you already have. Waiting in line becomes a chance to practice. Walking turns into walking meditation. Even washing dishes can become a moment of mindful presence.

Quick Solutions

- Start with just three conscious breaths
- Use existing activities as awareness anchors
- Remember: consistency matters more than duration

"I Keep Forgetting"

This is normal and part of the process. Each time you remember is a moment of awakening, not a failure.

Helpful Strategies

- Set gentle phone reminders
- Use physical cues (doorways, car keys) as practice triggers
- Be patient with yourself—building new habits takes time

"It Feels Artificial"

At first, intentionally practicing awareness might feel awkward or unnatural. This feeling decreases as the practices become more integrated.

Working with This

- Start with practices that feel most natural to you
- Remember that learning any new skill feels awkward initially
- Focus on the benefits you notice rather than the process feeling "right"

"My Mind Is Too Busy"

A busy mind doesn't block practice—it's what makes it meaningful.

Approaches

- Don't attempt to stop thoughts; simply observe the Loving Awareness that notices them

- Use physical sensations like breathing and walking as anchors when thoughts become intense
- Remember that the goal isn't having a quiet mind but cultivating a spacious relationship with whatever mind you have

"I Feel Spiritually Homesick All the Time"

This deep longing can actually become your most reliable doorway to practice.

Approaches

- Use the homesickness itself as a reminder to connect with Loving Awareness
- Practice recognizing that what you're homesick for is your own true nature
- Remember that this longing contains wisdom—it's pointing you toward what truly matters

The Ripple Effect: How Personal Practice Serves Others

When we establish a rhythm of engaged awareness, something remarkable happens: our presence becomes a gift to everyone we meet. As Dr. Michael discovered, we don't need to announce our practice or try to "help" others directly. Simply by being more grounded, present, and open-hearted, we create an atmosphere that allows others to access their own deeper resources—offering natural medicine for the spiritual homesickness that affects so many.

In Professional Settings

- Meetings are more productive when someone present is grounded and clear
- Conflicts tend to resolve when approached with calm awareness instead of reactivity
- Creativity flows more easily in environments that focus on the present moment

In Family Life

- Children feel safer and more regulated around adults who are present and calm
- Partners experience deeper intimacy when both people can be genuinely present
- Family stress lessens when at least one person stays connected to expanded Loving Awareness

In Community

- Grocery store clerks, bus drivers, and other service workers often respond positively to genuine presence
- Neighborhood interactions become warmer when approached with open-hearted awareness
- Social tensions can soften when met with curiosity rather than judgment
- Your natural presence offers healing medicine for the epidemic of spiritual homesickness affecting our communities

Technology and Engaged Awareness

In our digital age, technology can either fragment our attention or support our practice, depending on how we use it.

Skillful Use of Technology

- Set specific times for checking emails and social media rather than constant monitoring
- Use technology mindfully—notice when you're reaching for your phone out of habit vs. genuine need
- Create phone-free zones and times (meals, bedrooms, first hour of the day)
- Use apps or reminders as helpful tools, not replacements for real practice.

Digital Detox Practices

- Regularly disconnect, even for just an hour, to reconnect with immediate experience
- Experience time in nature without devices
- Have face-to-face conversations free of digital distractions
- Rediscover simple pleasures that don't involve screens

Noticing Progress in Engaged Awareness

Progress in engaged awareness isn't measured by how often you remember to practice, but by subtle shifts in how you meet life's challenges

Signs of Integration

- Increased resilience: Difficulties still arise, but you recover more quickly
- Greater presence: Others comment that you seem more "there" when with them
- Reduced reactivity: You pause more often before responding, especially in challenging situations
- Natural compassion: Care for others arises spontaneously rather than feeling effortful
- Improved relationships: People feel safer and more at ease in your presence
- Enhanced creativity: Solutions and insights emerge more naturally
- Deeper contentment: Satisfaction comes from being present rather than achieving goals
- Healing of spiritual homesickness: A growing sense of being at home in your own life and in the world

When Practice Feels Difficult

Some days, maintaining awareness feels effortless. Other days, it requires more intention. Both are normal parts of the journey.

During Challenging Periods:

- Return to the most basic practices (three conscious breaths)
- Remember that difficulty often precedes a breakthrough
- Seek support from others on similar paths
- Be especially gentle with yourself
- Trust that even "unsuccessful" attempts at practice are beneficial

Living the Questions

As you develop your own rhythm of engaged awareness, you might find yourself living with questions rather than having all the answers.

- How can I be both fully engaged and deeply peaceful?
- What does it mean to care without burning out?
- How do I stay open-hearted in a world that often seems harsh?
- What's the difference between spiritual bypassing and healthy detachment?
- How can I help heal the spiritual homesickness I see everywhere?

These questions themselves become part of the journey. Instead of seeking immediate answers, we can live with them, allowing our experience to slowly reveal deeper understanding.

The Ultimate Integration

The goal of engaged awareness isn't to become a perfectly mindful person who never gets triggered or loses presence. It's to build such familiarity with the field of Loving Awareness that we can return to it more and more quickly when we inevitably get lost in reactivity, worry, or old patterns—including the old pattern of spiritual homesickness.

Dr. Michael teaches us that returning to presence doesn't need perfect conditions. Even with hospital chaos, family demands, and global uncertainty, we can still reconnect with the expansive awareness that is our true home. Each return is a homecoming—not to a place, but to the vast, Loving Awareness that we are.

As you try these practices, remember you're not adding more to your to-do list. You're learning how to live your current life from a deeper, more connected place. The same activities—working, parenting, relating, resting—become ways to express awakened awareness instead of just chores to complete.

This is the promise of engaged awareness: not to avoid our human responsibilities, but to transform how we approach them. From this place, our lives become both deeply fulfilling and genuinely helpful to others—not because we're trying to help, but because presence itself is naturally healing and beneficial—offering medicine for the spiritual homesickness that affects so many in our time.

Creating Your Personal Practice

To close this chapter, take some time to consider how you might incorporate these practices into your personal life circumstances.

Questions for Reflection

- What are my natural transition points during the day where I could pause for brief awareness practices?
- What physical sensations or actions can act as anchors for staying present in the moment?

- How can my work or daily responsibilities become opportunities for engaged awareness?
- What realistic commitments can I make to myself about consistent practice?
- Who in my life could benefit from my greater presence and stability?
- How can I offer healing presence to those suffering from spiritual homesickness?

Creating Your Daily Rhythm

- Choose one morning practice that feels sustainable
- Identify 3-5 brief practices you can weave throughout your day
- Select one evening practice for integration and release
- Start small and gradually expand rather than overwhelming yourself initially
- Remember that the goal is consistency rather than perfection

The path of engaged awareness is fundamentally about realizing that the sacred isn't separate from the everyday—it's the Loving Awareness in which all ordinary experiences occur. As you become more familiar with this realization, your daily life transforms into both your practice and your offering to the world—healing medicine for our collectively spiritually homesick world.

CHAPTER 12

Bringing it Home—The Complete Integration

As we learn to live from Loving Awareness in our daily activities, something remarkable happens: our lives start to reflect wisdom and compassion instead of just personal survival strategies. Like Joanna Macy shows through her decades of service, when we anchor ourselves in the formless foundation of being, we find resources for engagement that we never knew we had—resources that can help heal our individually and collectively spiritually homesick world.

This practice offers healing for spiritual homesickness by completing the triple integration: personal healing becomes collective medicine as we learn to serve our spiritually homesick world from the inexhaustible source of Loving Awareness, recognizing our essential interconnectedness, and finding our authentic purpose in love's natural expression as service.

Rain ran down the large hospital windowpane as thick clouds enveloped the Berkeley hills on this cold, winter afternoon. Then, in her 94th year, Joanna looked frail in her hospital gown, and the many tubes hanging from her arm gave a sense of foreboding. Her labored breath sounded worrisome. Yet, her eyes were bright and fully alive, and her smile warmed up the room. This was two years before Joanna Macy would pass on in the summer of 2025.

"I'm so glad to be alive at this time," she said softly, each word requiring effort. "I'm so glad that we are together. Let's look out at the beautiful redwood trees," she continued, "I feel as though they're hugging us from both sides."

Michael, my husband, said, "Joanna, I feel the Earth is happy that you're still here."

"Yes, there are still things I want to do," she answered, smiling at us both, and turning to me, adding, "Let's do a meditation together."

I began the meditation with a felt sense of the body practice. We felt inward and outward, and into the resonance of the heart. From the fullness of the heart, we extended to the body as a whole once more, and then to the resonance of awareness itself.

"Feel awareness as body and body as awareness; awareness as heart and heart as awareness," I said.

Swiftly, our meditation expanded to the vast, ocean-like field of awareness itself. Joanna often spoke about the Field of Awareness, which she called "the mother of all wisdom and compassion," out of which spacious awareness and phenomena arise and return again.

"We are groundless ground," I continued, "we arise from it, and we dissolve back into it."

Joanna placed her hand on her heart and nodded gently. We sat together in silence, blissful and content, for a long while.

Even facing her own mortality, Joanna embodied full healing from spiritual homesickness. She had found her true home in the vast field of Loving Awareness, and this recognition allowed her to face even grave illness and possible death with peace and gratitude. Her presence was a living demonstration that when we heal our own spiritual homesickness, we become a healing presence for others.

The Wisdom of Service

Joanna Macy has been an environmental activist and scholar who advocated for the health and well-being of the Earth for over forty-five years. Although she was always acutely aware of the state of our world, including the existential threats of war, countless refugees, climate collapse, rising authoritarianism, and unraveling ecosystems, she reported that she still felt happy and at peace within herself.

"I'm so glad to be alive at this time so I can be helpful, so I can be part of it all," she whispered. "This gives me so much meaning."

Being aware of the struggles of the human condition can make us feel sad, bring us down, and leave us feeling overwhelmed. The huge suffering around us can break our hearts. However, what I see in Joanna and experience in myself is that when we can rest in awareness at least some of the time, we can stay present and loving even during tough times. It's as if our psychospiritual system has shifted from the small, scared personal ego-self to a bigger and broader view. This new outlook proves helpful in times of illness, personal trouble, and when we face the big challenges confronting our country and the world—including the epidemic of spiritual homesickness that affects so many.

Michael and I stood on either side of Joanna, who was sitting on her bed, as we looked out the window together. Just then, the rain started to clear, revealing the hills. Moments later, rays of sunshine streamed through the rain clouds.

"There's a rainbow!" Michael called out. Joanna jumped up from her bed and rushed closer to the window, smiling with delight. The rainbow shone brightly with neon colors—purple, orange, yellow, green, and blue. Then, faintly, we saw a shimmering double rainbow. Joanna leaned gently against me; her hand nestled into mine.

"Our world is a miracle," she said quietly.

Two weeks later, I was sitting with Joanna again at her home, where she was recovering from her chest infection. Although nearly 94 years old, she was very wise and clear, but physically frail. I told her about the book I was writing and my hopes to make Loving Awareness practices, which were previously difficult to access, available to everyone who wants to learn. She clapped her hands in delight.

"You're a Robin Hood, a spiritual caregiver. I love that!" She continued, "We're all in a world that's falling apart." She looked at me quite seriously. "These are dangerous times. What are we saving these practices for? It's now or never."

I asked Joanna how she can be so bright and high-spirited while also being so aware of the state of our world. She paused for a moment, then said, "You know I'm so grateful." As she looked around the room slowly, she added, "I'm grateful for this, and this, and this, and well, for all that's here, and that I'm still here, too."

"But where does your gratitude come from, Joanna?" I asked.

"I don't know!" she smiled. "It somehow just 'happened.' The world is spacious and more alive, more sacred now." With her moving hands, she gestured to show how lively and sparkly life felt. "I'm so grateful to be here and of service," she smiled again, timid and mischievous at the same time.

I thought to myself that perhaps her many years of service to others and our world, her spiritual path, and her decades of diligent practice came back to her as a blessing.

When spiritual practice and compassionate action come together, we show interdependence in our lives. Joanna loved the world, with all its beauty and pain. She understood and cared for our planet and its people, dedicating her life to helping others. I felt that the Earth loved her in return and did not want to let her go.

I loved Joanna dearly and have learned so much from her. There are three key lessons I've gained from her. First, it's possible to stay aware and empathize with others and our world without becoming depressed or burned out. Second, when we access Loving Awareness and open our hearts wide, we tap into a superpower that helps us stay resilient even in the darkest times. Third, if more of us embraced an attitude of gratitude and acted from this perspective, the world would be healthier and friendlier—and our collective spiritual homesickness could start to heal.

When Joanna passed away peacefully, she was still radiant with gratitude and care, more for others than for herself. Until the very end, she filled us with her wonderful energy of service and love. Now, we, her friends and students, need to figure out how carry Joanna's work forward and how to expand it in a way that fits contemporary needs. Joanna's work, along with future adaptations, will be healing medicine for our socially hurting, morally bankrupt and spiritually homesick world.

As we heal our own spiritual homesickness through complete integration of the triple medicine, we naturally become healing energies for our collectively spiritually homesick world. Joanna's life demonstrated the ultimate result: when personal healing turns into collective healing, service flows from boundless love.

Engaging with the World from Loving Awareness

A life dedicated to service and meditation changes us, helping us see old age, illness, and death in a different light. I have seen how one can face these "three messengers," as they are called in contemplative philosophy, with open hearts. Although spiritual practices of all kinds are helpful when dealing with life's uncertainties and challenges, those that help us to enter into Loving Awareness can make an important difference.

It seems especially important that we move beyond our idea of a separate self, of ego, of "my, me, mine," toward a broader sense of identity. When we see ourselves as both ocean and wave, as interconnected, inseparable, mutually dependent, and emerging together as awareness energy, we can face challenges with more resilience, grace, gratitude, and kindness.

Most importantly, this understanding offers gentle healing for spiritual homesickness. When we recognize our true nature as vast Loving Awareness, we realize we have never actually been separate from our true home. The longing that characterizes spiritual homesickness transforms from suffering into wisdom—it becomes recognition of our deepest nature, calling us back to itself.

The Integration of Practice and Life

There are three stages in incorporating Loving Awareness practices into our lives. During the first stage, we must carefully establish entrance to Loving Awareness with dedication, focus, and emptiness practice. In the second stage, we become used to Loving Awareness as our foundation. If we find that we have fallen out of Loving Awareness, intention helps us return to it. In the third stage, "Loving Awareness finds us." Suddenly, throughout our days, we discover ourselves in the glow of the flow of Loving Awareness, which has declared itself, unbidden.

Dr. Michael recently shared a powerful story with me. He was with a patient who was actively dying, surrounded by her family. The room was filled with grief and anxiety. Without consciously trying, he found himself resting in Loving Awareness. From this place, he was fully present with both the patient's suffering and the family's distress, while feeling a deep sense of peace. The words he spoke and the gestures he made came naturally from this state of awareness. Later, the family told him that his presence had created a sacred space, helping them to be fully present with their loved one in her final moments.

This is the result of consistent practice—not a detachment from life's struggles, but the ability to face them with presence, wisdom, and compassion that naturally arises when we learn to rest in our true nature. As Joanna Macy demonstrated through her life of engaged awareness, when we access the limitless Field of Care that is our true home, we discover an endless source of resilience, creativity, and love that can carry us through even the toughest times.

Tonglen for Fierce Compassion

Tonglen meditation, an ancient contemplative spiritual practice adapted by John Makransky, helps us be with what is painful in this world without being harmed or overwhelmed by personal grief—including the collective pain of our spiritually homesick world. When we feel another's suffering and extend well-wishing from a place of Loving Awareness, our experience will be heartfelt and simultaneously spacious and light. Feeling another's distress that touches our hearts ignites our compassion. Then we allow our concern for those who suffer to deepen our imagination, taking their pain into ourselves to offer care and support. Finally, we expand this wish to encompass all beings.

- Begin this practice by calling upon and taking refuge in your Field of Care. You can enhance this practice with a brief exercise of emptiness of self, which guides you into the spaciousness of awareness. When combined with the Field of Care and emptiness practice, this space can develop into one of Loving Awareness.

- Now, within this space of Loving Awareness, bring to mind the person or group you are concerned about, those who are in distress—including those suffering from spiritual homesickness. Against the background and supported by emptiness and the Field of Care, imagine taking the suffering in like a cloud into your heart. This cloud breaks open the shell of your self-preoccupation so that light can radiate out into the world.

- Feel that this radiant light shines out to those suffering. Imagine that this glow helps those who are hurting to find freedom, whatever that means to them. Let yourself feel the joy of having been part of their journey to freedom.

- Now, let this radiant light expand to all people and beings suffering in misery, enveloping them fully. Finally, think of everyone who feels the pain of living and dying, and visualize them now as light and free.

- In the final step, relax and release the visualization. Allow yourself to rest in the vast, unlimited field of awareness, becoming the ocean and the waves. Rest in the groundless ground of Loving Awareness, surrendering to depth with gratitude.

Tonglen Practice

Time needed: 10–15 minutes

Purpose: To cultivate compassion by breathing in the suffering of yourself or others, and breathing out relief, love, and healing—offering healing for spiritual homesickness by transforming our pain into medicine for others

Preparation

- Find a quiet place where you can sit comfortably, with your spine upright but relaxed
- Close your eyes gently or keep a soft, lowered gaze
- Take a few breaths, letting your body settle and your mind become still

Step 1: Connect with the Field of Care

- Recall a person, animal, or presence that embodies unconditional love for you
- Let yourself feel their care, warmth, safety, and acceptance
- Rest in this loving space for several breaths, allowing your heart to soften

Step 2: Resting in Emptiness

- Gently shift your attention to the space of awareness itself
- Notice how sensations, thoughts, and feelings arise and dissolve, like clouds passing through a vast sky
- Feel your sense of self dissolve in this limitless, boundless space
- Know the whole limitless, boundless field of awareness is suffused with warmth and love
- Rest here for a few breaths, sensing the boundless, clear nature of awareness

Step 3: Choose the Focus of Your Care

- Bring to mind someone who is suffering—it could be yourself, a loved one, a group, a country, or those who are experiencing a crisis of the soul, existential lostness, and a longing for a spiritual home
- Sense their pain or difficulty as best you can, without turning away or becoming overwhelmed

Step 4: Breathing in the Pain

- As you inhale, imagine drawing in their suffering in the form of dark, heavy smoke
- Let this smoke enter your heart, where it is met by the warmth and spaciousness you've cultivated
- Trust that your heart's compassion can hold and transform this pain

Step 5: Breathing Out Relief and Love

- As you exhale, imagine radiating out light, warmth, and ease—whatever those in distress most need
- See this energy flowing toward them, bringing comfort, healing, and freedom

Step 6: Continue the Cycle

- With each inhale, welcome their pain into the vast space of your heart
- With each exhale, offer love, relief, and blessing
- Let the rhythm of breath carry the practice naturally

Step 7: Expanding the Circle

- Gradually widen your focus to include more beings: friends, strangers, even those you find difficult
- Include those suffering from spiritual homesickness—the countless souls longing for meaning, depth, and authentic connection
- Inhale their sorrow, exhale your compassion and care
- Sense your unity with all life through this shared exchange

Integration

- Rest for a moment in the spacious, Loving Awareness you've touched
- Feel gratitude for your own capacity to love and for the connection you share with others
- Carry this openness into the rest of your day

Reflection: Feel this practice in your body, heart, and mind.

(On a Personal Note: see below)[37]

The Relevance for Our World

The practices of Loving Awareness are not just for monasteries or retreat centers—they are vital tools for managing our complex modern lives and addressing the biggest challenges facing our world, especially the epidemic of spiritual homesickness. In a reality where attention constantly fragments, where polarization divides communities, and where ecological anxiety shadows our future, these practices offer a way to stay rooted while fully engaging in life.

Parents find that even brief mindfulness exercises between responsibilities help them respond to their children's needs with more patience and presence. Healthcare workers discover that a moment of awareness before entering a patient's room enhances the quality of care they provide. Activists recognize that connecting with Loving Awareness before engaging in difficult conversations allows them to speak truthfully with both firmness and compassion.

The beauty of incorporating these practices into daily life is that they don't require us to escape our commitments—quite the opposite. They help us manage our responsibilities, relationships, and

---

[37] ***On a Personal Note:*** *Since my twenties, it has been a conundrum for me—how to hold the pain of others without getting overwhelmed or burning out. I found this question not only relevant for myself, but I also wondered how to convince others to be helpful and generous. In my peers and fellow citizens, I witnessed so much hesitancy and fear to get engaged with other suffering people. Tonglen convinced me to be an immensely useful practice. I found it particularly helpful to see myself as an aspect of a larger field of life, of awareness. This reminded me of St. Francis's "Make me an instrument of thy peace."*

Then it seemed helpful to me to imagine those who are suffering as well again. I tried this practice out, imagining Palestinians and Israelis. Imagining Palestinians planting their olive trees again, and harvesting as families, and imagining Israelis and Palestinians sleeping well, without fear of the other. Doing the practice like this reminded me of Dr. Martin Luther King's "I have a dream" speech, which is such a powerful vision.

challenges with more wisdom and resilience. Whether we're having a tough conversation with a colleague, hearing troubling news about the world, or just handling everyday stresses, these moments of awareness give us a refuge that's always available—a home we can return to amid life's storms.

This is what Dr. Michael and Joanna show through their lives—not spiritual bypassing or detachment from the world's suffering, but a brave willingness to stay present with both joy and sorrow, supported by the endless Field of Care that is our true nature. Most importantly, their lives demonstrate complete healing from spiritual homesickness—they have found their true home in Loving Awareness and naturally offer this medicine to others.

Fierce Compassion, Authentic Compassion

Joanna Macy has shown throughout her life's work that compassion can sometimes be fierce, honest, and direct. She has spoken out against nuclear war, championed human rights, and consistently defended the marginalized. This attitude is often referred to as "fierce" or "genuine" compassion. Its foundation is not based on hate or self-righteous anger. Instead, it means we are willing to support the highest potential in all humans rather than let them engage in harmful actions. Sometimes, we must confront others—whether it's a relative abusing drugs, a child hurting themselves or others, a person or group damaging the environment, or those who oppress and harm others. We recognize that all humans have the potential to do better, which is ultimately healthier for everyone. So, it's important to have the courage to confront those who cause harm.

This involves confronting the systems and attitudes that cause spiritual homesickness—such as the consumer culture that promises fulfillment through acquisition, digital technologies that fragment attention and genuine connection, political divisions that tear communities apart, and the destruction of natural environments that disconnect us from our larger home.

This is what my grandfather did when he confronted Nazi hooligans in 1933. The short-term outcome was not favorable for him, but he upheld an ethical and courageous stance for himself, his family, and his friends. He never regretted his brave action, as it gave him a sense of integrity and inspired hope in others. My grandfather was a quiet Christian man, a high-school teacher, known for his calm and kind demeanor. It is crucial that we don't act out of rage or a sense of superiority but rather with a gentle heart, standing up for what we believe is ethical and humane. Our meditations help us approach situations from a place of non-reactivity, while at the same time, we may feel our compassion deeply. Let us insist on depth and wholeness for all parties involved, with the intention and longing to advocate for a better world—a world where spiritual homesickness can be healed through authentic community, meaningful work, and recognition of our sacred nature.

Extending Love for All

I realized that my ability to live with fierce, authentic compassion and engagement is deeply connected to my capacity to receive love—to let it in, and to allow myself to be loved. *(On a Personal Note: see below)*[38] This ability to receive is closely linked to the gift of loving others. This remains true even when I disagree with or feel disturbed by them. The "Extending Love" meditation helped me expand my capacity for genuine friendliness and kindness toward others, even when they frustrate me.

It is important to first connect with a source of care and love, the Field of Care, and allow yourself to be genuinely receptive to it. We begin by accepting love for ourselves, which creates a stable foundation for truly offering love to others. Gradually, we can start to extend that energy outward. When starting this practice, choose someone you feel neutral about, rather than someone who triggers strong emotions. This approach allows you to learn the technique

---

[38] ***On a Personal Note:*** *These practices, as I said before, remind me so strongly of Dr. Martin Luther King's "I Have a Dream" speech. There is such a power in active hope, in having a vision or a dream, of refusing to be discouraged or defeated. "Discouraged" means that we lost our heart, our core. Therefore, I need these specific practices to keep my heart, my core, strong, and to stay joyful, with eyes wide open.*

without getting caught in familiar reactive patterns. Over time, you can expand your well-wishing and friendliness to those who are challenging for you. By recognizing that we all desire happiness and freedom from suffering—including freedom from spiritual homesickness—we acknowledge our shared humanity. This understanding makes it easier to radiate the energy of love outward in a more inclusive way.

Practice: Extending Love

(adapted from John Makransky)

Time needed: 10-15 minutes

Purpose: To enhance our true ability for universal kindness—finding your existential and spiritual home by recognizing our shared longing for love and meaning

Instructions:

Feel your body and breath

- Sit comfortably with your back straight, eyes softly looking downward or closed
- Allow awareness to flow from the thinking mind into the entire body
- Let your breath naturally emerge from this body sense of feeling and find its natural rhythm
- Feel the unified field of body, breath, and awareness, allowing your outbreath to draw you deeper into presence
- Sense how each breath naturally pulls you deeper into a calm presence

Feel your Field of Care

- Bring to mind your Field of Care surrounding you now

- This could be a loving moment with someone close to you, being in nature, with a mentor, or feeling the presence of a spiritual figure
- Allow yourself to be recognized as profoundly deserving of love, beyond any judgments or conditions
- Feel this loving energy starting to fill your entire being, warming you from the inside out
- Let this love fill every cell and every layer of feeling and emotion in your body
- Rest in the felt sense of being fully accepted and cherished deep within your being
- Let this loving energy start to flow through your entire being, especially into your heart, as if you were filled with soft sunlight

When something in you resists

- If any part of you resists or feels doubt, just give it space
- Without attempting to fix the feeling, welcome it with compassion
- Don't try to change this feeling—just acknowledge it with deep allowing

Extending love to another

- Now think of someone in your life, maybe someone you feel neutral or kindly towards
- While you continue to receive love from your caring environment, let the same energy flow through you to them
- Imagine yourself as an open window through which loving energy flows freely
- Allow this gentle light to fill their entire being, recognizing their profound dignity and worth
- Wish them well and recognize their full humanity beyond surface impressions

Extending love further and further

- If you feel ready, share this loving energy more broadly with those around you, even if they might be harder to like
- Include those who may be suffering from spiritual homesickness—those who seem disconnected, angry, despairing, or lost
- Know that this love and care are qualities of the great Field of Loving Awareness—limitless, boundless, inexhaustible, and always already present
- Let the flow of love guide you to recognize the inherent worth in yourself and all beings

Resting in boundless space

- Now fully relax into this space of warmth, acceptance, and loving care
- Let your heart and mind let go of all preconceived notions, opening gently like infinite space
- Rest in this unity of expansive awareness and love, letting everything just be

Reflection: Feel this practice in your body, heart, and mind.

This is a vital practice, not unlike physical therapy, that gently expands the capacity of our muscles and tendons. Be patient with yourself, and understand that with consistent practice, it will become progressively easier and even natural to include others in your loving care—including those suffering from their own forms of spiritual homesickness.

Returning Home to Awareness

Throughout this book, we have explored numerous pathways to awaken Loving Awareness—by focusing on the body and breath, engaging in emptiness practices, opening the heart, feeling our interdependence, and engaging ourselves in our world. We have discovered that awareness is not something we need to create or achieve; rather, it is our natural state—our true home to which we can return time and again.

As you close these pages and move forward on your journey, remember that the practices offered here are not just another item on your to-do list or a self-improvement project. They are invitations to recognize what has always been there, the vast, loving, intelligent field of awareness that is your true nature—the ultimate healing for spiritual homesickness.

In the words of Joanna Macy, "Our world is a miracle." When we rest in Loving Awareness, we can recognize this miracle even amid difficulties and suffering. We can respond to life's challenges from a place of being grounded, compassionate, and wise. We can fully engage in the work of healing ourselves and our world without becoming overwhelmed or burned out.

This is the gift of Loving Awareness—not an escape from life but a deeper, more loving, and wiser engagement with it. It is not a rejection of our humanity but an acceptance of our full potential as human beings. It does not mean turning away from the world's suffering but instead facing it with an open heart and a clear mind—offering healing medicine for our spiritually homesick world.

Our journey together through these pages ends here, but the journey of Loving Awareness continues moment by moment, breath by breath, for as long as we live. Each moment offers the chance to return to awareness, to love, to recognize our true nature, and to live from that perspective. Most importantly, each moment offers the opportunity to heal spiritual homesickness—both our own and that of others—by recognizing and sharing the love and meaning that is our birthright.

EPILOGUE

The Field of Love as Medicine for Our Time

"May I be the protector to all those without protection,
A leader, for all those who journey,
A boat, a bridge, a passage for all those desiring the further shore.

May the pain of every living creature be completely cleared away.
May I be the doctor and the medicine; may I be the nurse for all sick beings in the world,
until everyone is healed.

Just like space, and the great elements such as Earth, may I always support the life of all boundless creatures, until they pass away from pain.

May I also be the source of life for all the realms of varied beings that reach into the end of space. In this limitless spaciousness, is the play of compassion."

-Shantideva's Prayer

As we close this exploration of the Field of Love, we return to where we began—recognizing that spiritual homesickness, that deep ache for something more meaningful than our consumer culture offers, is actually the soul's recognition of its true nature calling itself home.

The practices in this book are not merely techniques for personal well-being but pathways to healing the collective disconnection of our time. When we learn to rest in Loving Awareness, we become medicine for an existentially bereft, scared, and spiritually homesick world—not by fixing others or changing external circumstances, but by embodying the love and awareness that is always available, always here, always our deepest home.

The Triple Medicine Fulfilled

Throughout this journey, we have discovered that spiritual homesickness arises from a threefold disconnection that requires integrated healing.

Healing disconnection from our true nature comes from realizing that awareness itself is inherently loving and endlessly resourceful. We don't have to force peace or love; instead, we must see that our deepest nature is the very peace and love we've been searching for.

Disconnection from others is healed by recognizing our fundamental interconnectedness—not as a philosophical idea but as a lived reality. When we see that all beings, this whole web of life, are waves on the same ocean of consciousness, service becomes not sacrifice but recognition. Then we become the ocean, become one with it, rest in it. Then our engagement emerges from this place of fullness.

Disconnection from meaningful purpose is healed when we realize that authentic service naturally arises from Loving Awareness rather than strained effort. Our work in the world becomes a spontaneous reflection of who we are, not something we have to force ourselves to do.

When these three recognitions become integrated, we don't just heal our own emotional disconnect and spiritual homesickness—we become healing medicine for others experiencing the same collective displacement.

A Message for Our Time

We live in times that call for spiritual rebels—people willing to be guided by love rather than fear, by wisdom rather than reactivity, by interconnection rather than separation. The practices in this book offer a systematic path for this transformation, moving us from spiritual homesickness to becoming the very medicine our world needs.

This isn't about becoming perfect. It's about discovering that our full humanity—including our capacity to feel pain for the world, to long for meaning, to care deeply about the future—can become our greatest strength when held within the field of Loving Awareness.

Living as Medicine

As you incorporate these practices into your daily routine, remember that you are not only healing your own spiritual homesickness but also helping to heal our collective displacement and alienation. Every moment you rest in Loving Awareness, every time you respond with compassion instead of reactivity, and every instance of genuine presence you offer—these become medicine for our lost and spiritually homesick world.

Your transformation helps others remember their own wholeness. Your presence allows others to relax their defenses. Your embodiment of Loving Awareness opens space for healing that reaches well beyond what you might imagine.

The Field of Love Expanding

The field of love is not something we create—it's something we recognize, embody, and offer. As more people discover this recognition, the field itself becomes more accessible to others. We are part of a growing network of human beings who are choosing love over fear, presence over distraction, service over selfishness.

This is how our individual healing becomes collective medicine. This is how we address not just personal heartache and spiritual homesickness but the epidemic of disconnection that affects our entire world.

Your Ongoing Journey

The practices in this book are not a final goal but a starting point. As you continue to explore and embody them, they will grow and change. What begins as a technique turns into a natural expression. What starts as personal practice becomes spontaneous service.

Trust the process. Be patient with yourself. Remember that healing heartbreak and spiritual homesickness—both yours and the world's—is not a project to finish but a way of being to embody, moment by precious moment.

The Invitation Continues

May all beings realize their true nature as Loving Awareness. May all beings be free from the suffering of existential heartbreak and spiritual homesickness. May all beings find their way home to the Field of Love that they are and have always been.

And may you, dear reader, know yourself as both the medicine and the healer, both the seeker and the sought, both the wave and the ocean—fully at home in the vast, Loving Awareness that is your deepest nature and the very source of healing for our ailing world.

The invitation is always there. The field of love is always accessible. Your true home is always here, waiting for you to realize what has never been absent—the Loving Awareness that you are.

In loving service to our awakening world,
Radhule Weininger

ACKNOWLEDGMENTS

This book emerged from a web of relationships and teachings that have sustained and shaped me for decades. I am profoundly grateful to each person who has been part of this journey.

To my husband, Michael: You have been my steady companion and inspiration through every step of this work. Your presence, wisdom, and unwavering support have made this book possible.

To my three adult children: Your extraordinary patience with me throughout this process has been a gift. Your editorial insights, technical expertise, and artistic support strengthened this work in ways only you could provide. This book is written for you and the world you carry forward.

To Joanna Macy: Your unflinching friendship has been a beacon. The intellectual rigor, spiritual depth, and fierce compassion you embodied have inspired me for years and continue to guide my understanding of what service means in these times.

To John Makransky: Your ongoing teaching has illuminated the path of sustainable compassion, and your trust in me as a teacher has been both humbling and empowering. Thank you for showing me how loving awareness can engage the world's suffering.

To Daniel P. Brown, Loch Kelly, and Dustin DiPerna: Your profound teachings on non-dual awareness have been invaluable. Each of you has offered keys that unlocked dimensions of practice and understanding I could not have discovered on my own.

To Jack Kornfield: Twenty years of your mentorship have shaped my path as a teacher and practitioner. Your wisdom, kindness, and encouragement have sustained me through countless moments of doubt and discovery.

To Joseph Goldstein: Your kindness and support in helping me find my way between mindfulness and non-dual teachings have been a gift. You showed me that these paths need not conflict but can deepen each other.

To my sangha and study companions: You have been my spiritual home. Your questions, practice, struggles, and breakthroughs—all of this has taught and challenged me to make these teachings more accessible and alive.

To Jennifer Leigh Selig: Your editorial wisdom and skill helped me find the clearest expression of these ideas. Thank you for seeing what this book could become and for helping me bring it into being through Mandorla Books.

Finally, to all who seek to heal spiritual homesickness—in yourselves and in our world—may these teachings meet that longing and honor the truth that the home we seek is already here, waiting in loving awareness.

REFERENCES

MAJOR INFLUENCES ON THIS WORK

Joanna Macy, PhD

Website: Joannamacy.net, Onbeing.org
YouTube: Joanna Macy, Honoring Our Pain for the World: Work that Reconnects
YouTube: Work That Reconnects, April 23, 24
Suggested Books:

- *World as Lover, World as Self: 30th Anniversary Edition,* Courage for Global Justice and Planetary Renewal, 2021, Parallax Press.
- *Active Hope,* Joanna Macy and Chris Johnstone, 2012, New World Library.

John Makransky, PhD

Website: Sustainablecompassion.org
Suggested Books:

- *How Compassion Works: A Step-By-Step Guide to Cultivating Wellbeing, Love, and Wisdom* (with John Condon), 2025, Shambhala.
- *Awakening Through Love: Unveiling Your Deepest Goodness,* 2007, Wisdom Publications.

Suggested Podcast:

- "Relational Meditation" on Paul Condon's *Mind & Live Podcast*, 2023.

Dustin DiPerna, MA

Website: Dustindiperna.org
Suggested Books:

- Editor of *Purpose Rising: A Global Movement of Transformation and Meaning*, 2017, Bright Alliance.

Loch Kelly, MSW

Website: Lochkelly.org

App: Mindful Glimpses: Awakening

Suggested Books:

- *Effortless Mindfulness Now: Awakening Our Natural Capacity for Focus, Freedom, and Joy,* 2018, Sounds True.
- *Effortless Mindfulness Now: Awakening Our Natural Capacity for Focus, Freedom, and Joy,*
- 2018, Sounds True
- *Shift Into Freedom,* 2015, Sounds True.

Daniel P. Brown, PhD

Website: Drdanielpbrown.com

Suggested Books:

- *Pointing Out The Great Way: The Stages of Meditation in the Mahamudra Tradition,* 2006, Wisdom Publications.
- *Transformations of Consciousness: Conventional and Contemplative Perspectives on Development,* 1986, Shambhala

Jack Kornfield, PhD

Website: Jackkornfield.com

Suggested Books:

- *Wise Heart: A Guide to the Universal Teachings of Buddhist Psychology*, 2009, Bantam.
- *A Path With Heart: A Guide Through the Perils and Promises of Spiritual Life,* 1993, Bantam
- *Seeking the Heart of Wisdom: Joseph Goldstein and Jack Kornfield,* 1987, Shambhala

Joseph Goldstein

Website: Dharma.org

Suggested Books:

- *Mindfulness: A Practical Guide to Awakening*, 2016, Sounds True.

- *Seeking The Heart of Wisdom: The Path of Insight Meditation*, 1987, Shambhala.

Dalai Lama

Website: Dalailama.org

Suggested Books:

- *Beyond Religion: Ethics For A Whole World,* 2012, HarperOne.
- *How To See Yourself As You Really Are*, 2007, Atria Books.
- *The Art of Happiness: A Handbook for Living,* 1998, Riverhead Books.

OTHER REFERENCES

Anonymous, *The Cloud of Unknowing,* 2009, Paraclete Press.

Aurobindo, Sri. *Isha Upanishad*, Gyan Books, 2024.

Bourgeault, Cynthia. *Eye of the Heart,* 2020, Shambhala.

-----*The Wisdom Jesus,* 2008, Shambhala.

Dass, Ram. *Be Love Now: The Path of the Heart*, 2010, HarperOne.

Eckhart, Meister. *The Complete Mystical Works of Meister Eckhart*, 2010, Herder & Herder.

Gibran, Khalil. *The Prophet,* 1971, Alfred A. Knopp.

Hanh, Thich Nhat. *No Death: Comforting Wisdom for Life, No Fear,* 2002, Riverhead Books.

James, William. *The Principles of Psychology,* 2024, Diamond Pocket Books.

Julian of Norwich. *The Complete Julian of Norwich*, 2009, Paraclete Press.

Kearney, Michael. *A Place of Healing (3rd edition),* Mandorla Books, 2026.

----- *Becoming Forest,* 2023, All Night Books

-----*A Nest in the Stream*, Parallax Press, 2018.

Merton, Thomas. *The Seven Story Mountain,* 1998, Harper One.

----- *Hidden Ground of Love,* 1993, Harcourt.

Salzberg, Sharon. *Loving Kindness: The Revolutionary Art of Happiness,* 2002, Shambhala Publications.

Schwartz, Richard. *Internal Family Systems,* 2019, Guilford Publications.

Shantideva. *The Way of the Bodhisattva*, 2006, PongoBooks.

Trungpa, Chögyam. *Cutting Through Spiritual Materialism*, 1987, Shambhala.

Weininger, Radhule. *Heartwork: The Path to Self-Compassion,* 2021, Shambhala.

-----*Heart Medicine: How to Stop Painful Patterns and Find Peace and Freedom,* 2016, Shambhala.

www.ingramcontent.com/pod-product-compliance
Lightning Source LLC
LaVergne TN
LVHW091037080826
845145LV00002B/528

9781950186624